Praying the Way

The Bible Reading Fellowship
15 The Chambers, Vineyard
Abingdon OX14 3FE
brf.org.uk

The Bible Reading Fellowship (BRF) is a Registered Charity (233280)

ISBN 978 0 85746 716 4
First published 2018
10 9 8 7 6 5 4 3 2 1 0
All rights reserved

Acknowledgements
Unless otherwise stated, scripture quotations are from the New Revised Standard
Version of the Bible, Anglicised Edition, copyright © 1989, 1995 by the Division of
Christian Education of the National Council of the Churches of Christ in the USA.
Used by permission. All rights reserved.

Scripture quotations marked REB are taken from the Revised English Bible, copyright
© Cambridge University Press and Oxford University Press 1989. All rights reserved.

Prayers in Praying with Mark previously published in *God's Passion: Praying with
Mark* (Darton, Longman and Todd, 2011), and prayers in Praying with Luke previously
published in *God's Embrace: Praying with Luke* (Darton, Longman and Todd, 2012).

Every effort has been made to trace and contact copyright owners for material used
in this resource. We apologise for any inadvertent omissions or errors, and would
ask those concerned to contact us so that full acknowledgement can be made in
the future.

A catalogue record for this book is available from the British Library

Printed and bound by CPI Group (UK) Ltd, Croydon CR0 4YY

To Graham,

Praying
the Way

with Matthew, Mark, Luke and John

God bless and keep you

Terry Hinks

Contents

Introducing the gospels

This collection of readings and prayers is an invitation to journey with the four gospel writers, as they share with us the precious pearl that is God's kingdom, revealed in the life and teaching of Jesus Christ. Each writer told the story of Jesus in their own distinct way, reflecting the sources and traditions they knew and the situations which they and their church communities faced. Each brought their own wisdom, background and gifts to bear as they shared the good news of Jesus, energised by God's Spirit. Their fourfold witness to Christ is a source of delight rather than concern and difficulty; their very differences give reality to their testimony. Ultimately there is only one gospel – the good news of Jesus Christ – but the four witnesses bring a more rounded, fascinating and dynamic picture of Christ than one storyteller could produce.

Each invites us to follow the way of Jesus. In the book of Acts, Luke describes the early Christian movement as those who belonged to 'the Way': Saul journeyed to Damascus, 'so that if he found any who belonged to the Way, men or women, he might bring them bound to Jerusalem' (Acts 9:2). 'The Way' has a whole variety of meanings within Acts and the New Testament as a whole, with deep roots in the Old Testament. It speaks both of God's initiative and of our human response.

First and foremost 'the Way' is God's rather than our own; it is God who reaches out to the world to bring rescue and liberation. Isaiah spoke of a new exodus, with the exiles in Babylon returning to Jerusalem, and the gospel writers took up this imagery as they reflected on the work of Jesus. Quoting from the book of Isaiah, they describe John the Baptist as the voice crying in the wilderness: 'Prepare the way of the Lord, make his paths straight' (e.g. Mark 1:3).

God opens the way for us all – the way to God and the way to truly live. In Jesus, the Son of God, the Word made flesh, God dwells with humanity, having made a way into the world. Luke's great song of Zechariah describes the coming of Jesus as a new dawn for humanity, giving 'light to those who sit in darkness and in the shadow of death, to guide our feet into the way of peace' (Luke 1:79).

The dawn does not come without cost. Jesus is recognised as one who teaches the way of God, but this does not prevent his being rejected by those with power or position to lose. The way of Jesus becomes the way of the cross. At a critical moment in the gospels Jesus turns his face to Jerusalem and begins to speak of the rejection, suffering and death he will face there. Yet the way of the cross is ultimately transformed into the way of victory as, raised to new life on the third day, Christ breaks the bonds of death and hatred. That evening he walks unrecognised with two disciples on the road to Emmaus and shows himself risen and alive as he shares bread with them. They recall how their hearts were burning within them as he talked to them on the road (see Luke 24:13–35). The way of life is open ahead of them, a life to be lived and shared with the world.

All this is God's doing and the gospel writers emphasise the centrality of God's kingdom and the person of Jesus, contrasting this with the doubts, misunderstanding, failures and inadequacies of his disciples. John sums up the message in the great 'I am' statements as he meditates on the person of Jesus: Jesus is 'the way' (John 14:6), making the unseen God known and opening God's heart to all who trust in him.

The Way is of God's making, but humanity is challenged to respond and to enter this way. Key to the gospel message is Jesus' invitation, 'follow me'. For the fishermen and the many others it meant their world's being turned upside down, with a new way of looking at God, the world and themselves, and a new way of living too. That following required trust, risk and love. It involved listening deeply to Jesus' teaching and learning from his every action. Mistakes and misunderstandings became the opportunity to discover their need, experience forgiveness and take to heart the challenge to trust more in Jesus. They and all potential disciples are invited to follow the difficult way that leads to life and to build on rock, rather than shifting sand.

As we prepare to embark on our reading of the four gospels and to pray with them, it is good to reflect on the way we will be taking. Prayer at its simplest is about giving loving attention to the God who is the source and goal of all life. As we pray with the gospels we give our attention to Jesus, and listen for that word of God that was made flesh in him. We seek God's Spirit to enlighten and connect his story with our own situation and the world in all its wonder and terror. We choose to follow the Way and pray:

> The gospel comes to me, full of choices:
> the choice to follow or to stay,
> to walk the broad path that may destroy my soul
> or the narrow way that leads to life;
> the choice to be built on rock or on sand;
> trust or fear, love or hate,
> blessing or curse, life or death;
> the choice to live by outward appearance
> or the inward naked heart,
> to respond to need or to turn away.
>
> Living Lord, help me to choose life,
> not once, but each and every day.
> Show me how to pray and walk your way
> not tomorrow or yesterday,
> but now.

1

Praying with Matthew

How do we best pray the way with Matthew? One of the great keys to prayer in Matthew's gospel lies at the heart of the sermon on the mount (Matthew 6:5–15). It begins by warning against parading our prayerfulness, but then goes deeper with the instruction to go 'into your room and shut the door and pray to your Father' and not to heap up 'empty phrases as the Gentiles do' (Matthew 6:5–8). These four verses are unique to Matthew and lead on to the giving of the Lord's Prayer, in the form Christians use to this day.

The verses are both beguiling and challenging in their directness and simplicity. Here Jesus gives the three entry points into true prayer as being space apart, stillness of heart and trust of God, the one who knows our need. All these are hard to achieve in our frantic 21st-century society, where technology provides a huge umbilical tube to keep us constantly connected, where we are bombarded with an unceasing flow of words and images that remain in our minds long after we turn off our televisions or computers, and where trust is often in short supply. Matthew's Jesus speaks of a room where the door can be shut, a storeroom for treasure, a place of safety; Elisha 'closed the door... and prayed to the Lord' (2 Kings 4:33). Here is a place of the heart, a place to encounter the God who is in secret and sees in secret, a place where one's motivation is truly exposed.

This is the groundwork necessary to prepare to pray, to be in the presence of the one who sees into the heart. Our praying is constantly in danger of degenerating into an exercise of self-justification and self-importance, into that hypocrisy that Jesus confronts so brutally in his attack on paraded piety. So we are challenged to enter the room of prayer and shut the door, yet assured that the room is not empty – God is present.

Matthew underlines this by breaking the threefold teaching on secret piety (almsgiving, prayer and fasting) to include teaching on prayer itself. After encouragement not to babble, Jesus gives his disciples a way of praying that is a series of petitions addressed to 'Our Father in heaven'. The Lord's Prayer is, in effect, the pinnacle and centre of Jesus' first collection of teaching. It begins 'Our Father in heaven' (Matthew 6:9), unlike the simpler 'Father' in Luke's version (Luke 11:2), to emphasise the communal dimension of prayer. Matthew has a particular concern for the life of the Christian community and is the only gospel to use the word 'church'. Even alone we pray in the company of God's people; if nothing else, God's reality as 'our Father' connects us together.

The balance of the prayer as Matthew records it is perfect, with three petitions focusing on God's name, kingdom and will and three petitions focusing on our bread, our wrongs and our struggles. Anthony Bloom likens the prayer to a series of ripples spreading from where a pebble falls into a pond, the centre of the circle being 'Our Father in heaven'. This careful construction reflects the Jewish traditions from which Jesus and Matthew himself came. Three times Jesus' followers are to ask for God's purposes to be fulfilled; then and only then do they turn to their own needs and challenges. This is a challenging way to enter prayer, but a necessary antidote to the self-help agendas of our own times. 'Strive first for the kingdom of

God and his righteousness' (Matthew 6:33) and then the rest will follow.

Prayer is always bound up with action. We pray so that we may live more according to the will of God, more in tune with the kingdom to come. We pray in dependence to God for our day-to-day lives, our very sustenance. We pray for forgiveness for the ways we have acted at odds with the teaching of Jesus and for help to forgive those who have wronged us. We pray for strength and wisdom in the face of trial, temptation and evil, praying for ourselves and others. Praying flows into living, and living is reflected upon in prayer. It expresses our utter reliance on the grace of God, the faithful presence of 'God with us'. Matthew assures us that this faithful presence will not fail, ending his gospel with Jesus' assurance, 'I am with you always, to the end of the age' (Matthew 28:20).

1   The surprising God

Matthew 1:1–25

'... and they shall name him Emmanuel', which means, 'God is
with us.'
MATTHEW 1:23

Jesus, Son of Abraham,
we worship you in word and silence.
We will not forget
your deep roots in the Jewish story,
fulfilling the Hebrew scriptures
and the promise of blessing
made to an elderly couple
long ago.

Jesus, Son of David,
we worship you in word and silence.
We will not forget
that you are the Messiah, the Christ,
fulfilling the longing of Israel
for a just and gentle ruler
for all nations.

Jesus, Son of Mary,
we worship you in word and silence.
We will not forget
the woman who carried you in her womb,
vulnerable yet strong,
bearing hope for us all.

Jesus, Son of Joseph,
we worship you in word and silence.
We will not forget the one
whose compassion and vision
protected your mother and you
from scandal or worse.

Jesus, Son of God,
we worship you in word and silence.
We will not forget
your presence with us always
as God with us
in the very heart of our living.

2 I shall not pass by

Matthew 2:1–23

**'A voice was heard in Ramah, wailing and loud lamentation,
Rachel weeping for her children…'**
MATTHEW 2:18

I shall not pass by this story
of evil, pain and grief,
a tyrant's rage
and an order to destroy,
obeyed without mercy:
a story of death when life had hardly begun
and the agony of loss that none can quench.

I shall not pass by this story,
echoed in every generation
in genocide and holocaust,
in gas chambers and ethnic cleansing,
Rwandan village, Armenian town
and Nazi concentration camp.

I shall not pass by.
The tears of so many overwhelm me.
I can only look to the child,
who escaped for a time
but not for very long.
When the hour came
he entered anguish and darkness,
a lonely death amid hatred and fear.
I can only look at his wounds,
the wounds of all humanity,
and pray, 'Lord, have mercy.'

3   The Beloved

Matthew 3:1–17

And a voice from heaven said, 'This is my Son, the Beloved, with whom I am well pleased.'
MATTHEW 3:17

Come immense, amazing God.

Come as the water of life,
immersing this world with your goodness,
turning our lives towards your kingdom,
our hearts and minds
to a new way of thinking
and a new way of being.

Come as the fire of truth,
exposing our presumption and complacency,
confronting the world's corrupt powers with your light
and our fruitless greed with your simple grace.
Yet in your fierce judgement,
do not forget your mercy.

Come as the Spirit of love,
freeing us from all that binds us,
drawing us into your kingdom way,
showing us that we too can be your beloved sons and daughters,
to walk the way of Jesus and delight your heart.

4   Wilderness struggle

Matthew 4:1–11

Jesus said to him, 'Away with you, Satan! for it is written, "Worship the Lord your God, and serve only him."'
MATTHEW 4:10

God of the wilderness,
in the name of Jesus,
who hungered in the desert,
we pray for humanity today.
We hold before you
those who hunger for food and justice.
We do not ask you to change stones into bread,
but to speak your living word,
to touch hardened hearts and burdened spirits,
to release the oppressed from the systems we create,
that the bounty of the earth may be shared by all.

God of the wilderness,
in the name of Jesus,
who held true to your living word,
we pray for your people today.
We do not ask for a magician's wand to keep us from all harm,
but a deep courage and perseverance,
the faith that will change lives and see us into your kingdom.
And when we hear your word,
give us the wisdom to hear it well
and not twist it for our own comfort and security.

God of the wilderness,
in the name of Jesus,
who resisted all evil and temptation,
we pray for the powerful of our world,
those whose words and actions affect so many.
We ask you to guard all from false pride or twisted vision,
the worship of power and wealth itself,
the delusion of being self-made.
For you alone are God,
the living God to be worshipped for evermore.

5   Light dawns

Matthew 4:12–25

From that time Jesus began to proclaim, 'Repent, for the kingdom of heaven has come near.'
MATTHEW 4:17

God of every place and every journey,
we thank you for the road Jesus travelled,
    from Bethlehem to Jerusalem,
    from Galilee to every nation.
We thank you for his identity as
    a child of Bethlehem,
    a refugee in Egypt,
    a carpenter in Nazareth,
    a son immersed in the Jordan,
    a man tested in the wilderness,
    and a travelling preacher
    around the villages of Galilee,
    reaching out to those on the very edges of your grace.
We thank you for the message he proclaimed,
a kingdom without boundaries or flag or force.
We thank you for the crowds
who followed him seeking help and healing
and the fishermen he called,
    to come with him,
    to follow his way,
    to share his kingdom work.
May we be part of his story today,
sharing his journey,
his life, here and now.

6   Beginning with blessing

Matthew 5:1–16

'Blessed are the poor in spirit, for theirs is the kingdom of heaven.'
MATTHEW 5:3

So, Lord Jesus,
this is how you begin,
not with accusations
or condemnation,
not with plans
or strategies.
You begin with your blessing,
on the poor ones,
the broken ones,
the unnoticed ones,
the longing ones.
You point us in a new direction,
calling humanity to be
hungry for change,
hungry for justice,
hungry for peace.
In our discontented
and merciless times,
speak your strange blessing.
Give us that purity and simplicity,
that singleness of heart,
that depth of compassion,
which will open our eyes to the God with us today
and bring us close to the kingdom of heaven.

7 Dig deep

Matthew 5:17–48

Jesus said: 'You have heard that it was said… But I say to you…'
MATTHEW 5:21–22, 27–28, 31–32, 33–34, 38–39, 43–44

Dig deep, Lord Jesus, dig deep into our hearts.
Blow apart our
self-satisfied
self-righteous
self-centred
claims to goodness
with your piercing words.

Purify our relationships
of every element
of use or abuse,
every crumb of anger,
every glimpse of false passion.

Empty our mouths
of the words that twist the truth
and our minds
of bitter thoughts.

Turn our lives around
by your cross-bearing love:
the love that does not count the cost,
the love that does not seek revenge,
the love that reaches out
far beyond the cosy inner circle
to those we count our enemies,
to those we do not count at all.

8   The ceaseless babble

Matthew 6:1–18

**'When you are praying, do not heap up empty phrases as the
Gentiles do.'**
MATTHEW 6:7

The ceaseless babble of our prayers
rises up to you, God of all:
    our cries for help,
    our angry shouts,
    our longing dreams,
    our thanks,
    our praise,
    our hopes,
    our fears.

Yet will you hear your people, God of all?
Will you listen for our voice?
In hearts stilled
and tongues turned to silence,
in minds exposed to grace
and souls in secret,
there you listen, Father of us all.
There we meet you,
as vibrant life and utter truth.
There you meet us,
with grace and joy.

9   One-hearted living

Matthew 6:19–34

**'But strive first for the kingdom of God and his righteousness,
and all these things will be given to you as well.'**
MATTHEW 6:33

Such powerful forces lay claim upon my life.
I am battered by all those voices
that lay siege around my soul,
all the adverts pointing me
this way and that,
all the research projects and campaigns,
saying one thing, then another,
all the experts, all the reporters,
all the politicians, all the commentators,
arguing one case and then the next.
And those sterile voices within me,
shifting with the sands,
those wants that become needs,
those good things that take over.
Such powerful forces lay claim upon my life.

Yet you, the source of life,
are the true centre of all.
In you, all things find their rightful place.
With you, life makes sense.

10   Removing the log

Matthew 7:1–12

'Why do you see the speck in your neighbour's eye, but do not notice the log in your own eye?'
MATTHEW 7:3

God of simple truth,
we thank you for the words of Jesus,
the strange pictures that still
work their way into our minds and souls.

We thank you for the image of the log stuck in an eye,
an uncomfortable reminder
of our careless judgement of others
and our blindness to our own distorted seeing.
  Open our minds, clear our vision,
  give us truer understanding and wider compassion.

We thank you for the image of the pearls fed to the pigs,
an unsettling reminder of the ways we waste our souls,
using the best of our talents and our curiosity
on things that are not important.
  Open our minds, clear our vision,
  give us truer understanding and wider compassion.

We thank you for the image of a parent
feeding a child with a snake or a stone,
at odds with our most basic instincts,
an upside-down reminder of our need to trust you
as your children today.
  Open our minds, clear our vision,
  give us truer understanding and wider compassion.

With these striking pictures, turn our lives around,
that what we would want and pray for ourselves,
we may do for others.
So we ask this prayer not simply for ourselves
but for all humanity, in the name of Jesus,
your gracious image made flesh.

11   Act on it

Matthew 7:13–29

'Everyone then who hears these words of mine and acts on them will be like a wise man who built his house on rock.'
MATTHEW 7:24

I will travel your road today, Lord Jesus,
though the path may be hard
and the obstacles many.
I will travel your way,
that life that is full
of grace and goodness.

I will plant my life in you, Lord Jesus,
to bear that fruit,
that love and joy and peace,
I see in your very being.

I will build my dwelling, my home,
on your words, Lord Jesus,
the rock that cannot be swept away
by life or death,
by success or failure,
by power or weakness.

Walking your way,
planted in you,
built on your word,
save me from self-destruction,
and lead me to life,
eternal and true.

12   He bore our diseases

Matthew 8:1–17

This was to fulfil what had been spoken through the prophet Isaiah, 'He took our infirmities and bore our diseases.'
MATTHEW 8:17

God, the source of all wholeness,
the carrier of true health,
we thank you for all who bear
the cost of healing today,
reflecting in their skill and work,
their care and touch,
the kingdom work of Jesus
to bring health and wholeness,
hope and renewed life,
to your world here and now.

We thank you for surgeons repairing distorted skin,
doctors listening and diagnosing illnesses,
nurses responding to many needs,
researchers probing new medicines.
We thank you for social workers giving time,
carers washing those who are so frail,
volunteers bringing cups of tea,
managers balancing budgets,
friends showing their love,
family shedding tears.
We thank you for chaplains sitting at the bedside
and pastoral workers sharing the bread of life,
for prayers offered simply
and candles lit.

God of heights and depths,
be close to all whose pain is unbearable,
whose journey has entered the darkest place
or who hold a loved one's hand one last time.
Take their dis-ease upon yourself,
and bring that wholeness,
which is yours alone.

13   Confronting chaos

Matthew 8:18–34

'Lord, save us! We are perishing!'
MATTHEW 8:25

Lord, save us! We are perishing!
We drown in the sea of words and ideas,
voices shouting such varied messages,
lives pointing such different ways.
Fears crowd in on us –
the fear of the stranger, the random crime,
the pervasive virus, the disaster around the corner;
fears for ourselves, for our families,
for our communities, for our world.
Lord, for all our scientific prowess,
all our technological achievement,
nature cannot be controlled.
Teach us humility before its power.
Give us courage in the storms,
in the chaotic moments of life,
to free ourselves from the fears that bind us,
to find our way to your point of stillness,
to know creation as held in your hand
and to stay with you to the end.

14   Follow me

Matthew 9:1–17

As Jesus was walking along, he saw a man called Matthew sitting at the tax booth; and he said to him, 'Follow me.' And he got up and followed him.
MATTHEW 9:9

Disruptive Jesus,
you point to me,
in loving invitation,
piercing challenge
and life-giving promise.
You will not turn away.
You offer grace beyond measure,
blessings that cannot be counted.
You are the friend,
here to lift me to my feet.
You are the doctor,
here to heal my soul.
You are the bridegroom,
here to offer your love.
You point to me.
You call me to follow,
not in the past or in the future,
but in this very moment,
my here and now.

15   Great compassion

Matthew 9:18–38

When he saw the crowds, he had compassion for them, because they were harassed and helpless, like sheep without a shepherd.
MATTHEW 9:36

In a world of deep desperation,
how shall we speak of your great compassion?
How shall we reach out to touch your healing cloak?

In a world where too many die young,
how shall we bring new hope and life?
How shall we see each human being
with your gracious eyes?

In a world drowning in words and ideas,
facts and opinions, spin and slander,
how shall we show you as the shepherd king,
seeking out the lost, binding up their wounds,
carrying them on your shoulders,
leading them to safety?

Lord, call your people to action,
to the hard work of harvesting,
the costly business of mending lives,
opening eyes, touching wounds,
pointing to your kingdom,
where the harassed find help,
the lost find hope,
the sick find love.

16   Unconditional gospel

Matthew 10:1–42

'You received without payment; give without payment.'
MATTHEW 10:8

There can be no marketing of the gospel,
God of utter grace.
No conditions set or exchange made.
It is a gift without price,
entering our lives
to transform all we say or do,
everything we see or hear or touch.
It is a reality given solely by you, the giving God.

As we have received from you,
without charge or bribe,
so may we be generous in our giving.
May we share your good news, lived out in Jesus,
without agenda or subtext,
but simply because it is too good
to keep to ourselves.

God, our gracious Father and tender Mother,
give us your Spirit,
to free our tongues,
to speak graciously in the name of Jesus,
to hold to love in the face of hatred,
    faithfulness in the face of betrayal,
    peace in the face of conflict,
    welcome in the face of rejection,
    light in the face of darkness,
    truth in the face of distortion,
    hope in the face of judgement,
    life in the face of dying.

17   Come to me

Matthew 11:1–30

**'Come to me, all you that are weary and are carrying heavy
burdens, and I will give you rest.'**
MATTHEW 11:28

'Come to me, come to me,'
you say,
yet stubbornly I go my
own way.
'Come to me, come to me,'
you say,
yet foolishly I stand outside,
too proud to enter your presence,
too preoccupied to sense your call,
too clever to know my deep need.
Yet still,
'Come to me, come to me,'
you say.
And come I will.
I shall recognise the burdens I carry
and place them at your feet.
I shall look into
the restlessness of my heart
and find in you true rest.
I shall take my place among your workers,
sharing that load which you carry this day,
echoing that call to all humanity.
'Come to me, come to me,'
you say, 'learn my way,
for I am with you always,
to the end of all time.'

18   Standing alongside Jesus

Matthew 12:1–50

'For whoever does the will of my Father in heaven is my
brother and sister and mother.'
MATTHEW 12:50

We will stand with you, Lord Jesus.
When religion becomes a tool of oppression
rather than an instrument of mercy,
we will stand with you, the merciful one.
When rules become excuses to do nothing
and good people stay silent,
we will stand with you, in your goodness.
When the powerful conspire against you
and the weak are left on the scrapheap,
we will stand with you, the crucified one.
When the voiceless millions cry out
for food and health, hope and peace,
we will stand with you,
for you are with them in their suffering.
When the angry despise you
and the selfish turn their backs,
we will stand with you, the forgiving one.
When the world demands proof of your reality,
signs of your power today,
we will stand with you, the one who was buried,
yet rose again and meets us now.

For you are greater than Jonah and his sea monster.
You are greater than Solomon with all his wealth.
You are greater than all the powers that claim to rule,
all the names that parade their own stardom,
all the knowledge of our times.

For in you, we see true goodness.
In you, we see God.
In you, we see humanity,
as it can truly be,
brothers and sisters, made one in you.
We will stand with you, Lord Jesus.
Fill us with your Spirit.
Show us your way.

19   Dull hearts, closed minds

Matthew 13:1–43

**'For this people's heart has grown dull, and their ears are hard
of hearing, and they have shut their eyes…'**
MATTHEW 13:15

God of every living seed,
we thank you for the life that surrounds us
and the life that is within us.
We thank you for your life-giving word,
fertile, active and vibrant,
at the beginning of all beginnings
and in our time and space.
Forgive us when we have become deaf to your word,
when the business in hand closes our hearts to you.
Forgive us when disputes in your church
block out your living voice.
Forgive us when we mistake our words
for your creative word,
our fixed thoughts
for your true will.
Forgive us our dullness, our slowness, our hardness of heart.

God who made the mustard seed,
plant once more your seed of grace
in our lives today,
that your life may grow within us,
to heal, to lead, to live.

20   The pearl

Matthew 13:44–58

'Again, the kingdom of heaven is like a merchant in search of fine pearls; on finding one pearl of great value, he went and sold all that he had and bought it.'
MATTHEW 13:45–46

I quieten my mind and still my heart
and look at the pearl without price,
gloriously rare and beautiful,
natural and wild,
hidden among so many imitations.
This is your kingdom, God of grace,
generous love poured out in all its glory.

I quieten my mind and still my heart
and look at what I must do,
what I must be,
to take this precious pearl to heart,
to centre my life not on myself
or the expectations of others,
but on that generous love,
your kingdom, God of grace.

I quieten my mind and still my heart
and receive your wondrous gift,
with thanks and hope and joy.

21   They went and told Jesus

Matthew 14:1–21

His disciples came and took the body and buried it; then they went and told Jesus.
MATTHEW 14:12

We come and tell you, Jesus,
all that has happened this day,
in our lives and the life of our world.
We tell you of the joys and wonders,
stars shining brightly in the dark sky,
mountains reaching up into the clouds
and children playing in a park.
But there is more on our hearts.
We tell you the horrors of our world.
Young men and women gunned down in ordinary streets
and those who would destroy everything
in the name of their god.
We tell you of children abused and ruined,
lives that have hardly begun.
We tell you of atrocity after atrocity,
injustice built on injustice,
and our hearts grow weary,
our hopes and dreams tarnished by this world.
We come and tell you, Jesus,
and you take us to one side,
repairing our hearts and our hopes.
You bring us to a place of stillness.
You show us your love for humanity,
person by person.
You feed us and invite us to feed others,
filling us with life, made new.

22 Sacred ground

Matthew 14:22–36

And after he had dismissed the crowds, he went up the mountain by himself to pray. When evening came, he was there alone.
MATTHEW 14:23

Great I Am, we thank you
for those places where we can move
from doing and planning and striving
to being, simply with you.
We thank you for the hills of Galilee
with the lake below,
the sacred ground on which Jesus stood
and prayed to you.
We thank you for his vibrant presence,
driving out fear and terror
and bringing courage
to every shaking heart,
your 'I am' in flesh and blood.
Lead us to the sacred ground
of our own place and time,
the hills and lakes,
rooms or spaces,
where we can be, simply with you.
Remove our shoes of anxiety,
false pride and paralysing doubt,
and lead us, step by step,
as if walking on water,
to inch falteringly
into your kingdom,
for the sake of Jesus,
your true child,
your 'I am' for us.

23   Shameless prayer

Matthew 15:1–39

He answered, 'It is not fair to take the children's food and throw it to the dogs.' She said, 'Yes, Lord, yet even the dogs eat the crumbs that fall from their masters' table.' Then Jesus answered her, 'Woman, great is your faith!...'

MATTHEW 15:26–28

Where will your Spirit take us next,
God of all that lives?
Surely every barrier that divides
must be broken,
every human being welcomed to your feast,
as part of your whole creation.
The names by which whole races are demeaned
must be forgotten.
The labels we place on others must be thrown away.
Even your Spirit-filled child, Jesus,
had to learn your lesson,
that all are welcome at your table
and all can claim a share,
not of discarded scraps,
but the bread of heaven.
We thank you for all he learnt that day
from the unnamed woman of Canaan,
whose desperate prayer and sharpened wit
touched him to the core.
And we thank you for all he taught,
from his deepest being,
of your overwhelming compassion and glorious grace,
there to feed hungry humanity,
in all its messy complexity and desperate need.
Renew the core of our being
by your Spirit at work today.

24 A sign, a word, a way

Matthew 16:1–28

Then Jesus told his disciples, 'If any want to become my followers, let them deny themselves and take up their cross and follow me. For those who want to save their life will lose it, and those who lose their life for my sake will find it.'
MATTHEW 16:24–25

LIVING GOD,
you give us a sign,
THE BREAD,
broken and shared.
You give us a word,
THE CHRIST,
with us and for us.
You give us a way,
THE CROSS,
to follow each day.
By your Spirit,
give us eyes to see,
ears to hear,
strength to live,
CHRIST TODAY.

25   Mountain light and mustard-seed faith

Matthew 17:1–27

**But Jesus came and touched them, saying, 'Get up and do not
be afraid.'**
MATTHEW 17:7

You have set us free,
you, the one who shows your face
in the story of Jesus.
Your dazzling brightness
in mountain glory
has lightened our lives.
Your word of love
spoken then and now
has taken from us those deep fears
that haunt our lives today.
Your fierce grace
has confronted all that dehumanises
and degrades, and has given hope.
Your life given and raised in Christ
has released us to be your children.
So we pray that this day
we may live in your light,
knowing your tender touch,
your generous mercy,
in all we see and say,
all we think and do.
Raise us to our feet,
freed and thankful,
to live life,
new and true.

26 Children and sheep

Matthew 18:1–35

**'Truly I tell you, unless you change and become like children,
you will never enter the kingdom of heaven.'**
MATTHEW 18:3

God of all creation,
we thank you for sheep,
ready to be counted,
not to send us to sleep,
but to waken us
to your kingdom ways.
We thank you for your searching love,
reaching out to all who stumble,
all who struggle in life,
all who go stubbornly
along their own way,
in their own crumbling strength,
forgetting their good shepherd,
ignoring their connection
with others on the way.

God of all humanity,
we thank you for all
that reconnects people,
one with another,
and all that enables
forgiveness to take place.
We thank you for every glimpse
of that presence of Christ
found where two or three
gather in his name.

27   Sex and money

Matthew 19:1–30

'Have you not read that the one who made them at the beginning "made them male and female"?'
MATTHEW 19:4

God whose image we bear,
male and female, straight and gay,
rich and poor, young and old,
we pray for the healing of humanity.
We hold before you
all whose relationships are under strain
or have become bitterly broken,
and we pray too for those preparing for commitment
and those living out love, day by day.
We hold before you
every child who suffers
neglect or violence or abuse,
and we pray too for children
whose lives are happy and fulfilled.
We hold before you
those whose lives are blighted
by debt or poverty,
and those in captivity
to all they think they possess.
We pray too for those
who find joy in simplicity
and those who are learning to give.
Teach us all the gift of humanity.
Help us to seek out your image
in ourselves and others
and share that kingdom vision
where all can celebrate the earth's bounty
and heaven's joy.

28 Upside-down kingdom

Matthew 20:1–34

'It will not be so among you; but whoever wishes to be great among you must be your servant, and whoever wishes to be first among you must be your slave.'

MATTHEW 20:26–27

There can be no comparison with you,
the one who gives all life and hope and love.
No words can truly describe you.
No statements of belief define you.
No human faith contains you.
Stories told long ago speak best of you today.
Your master storyteller continues his work
with the tale of a generous employer drawing people into work
and his own narrative of a crucified king,
a servant lord and life-giver.
All the petty hierarchies we have built
will crumble before you.
The powerful will bow before your cross.
You, the one who gives life and hope and love,
will shatter all our attempts to use you,
to manipulate you for our own ends,
in the power games we play,
the bullying in the name of the Almighty,
the claims we make for our place in heaven.
Those who think themselves first will come in last.
The stumbling and disabled will win the race.
The dumb and voiceless will shout your praise.
The hungry and helpless will be paid in full.
The distressed and dying will receive eternal life.
Thank you, the one and only one,
beyond comparison, beyond compare.

29   Donkey-riding Messiah

Matthew 21:1–17

The crowds that went ahead of him and that followed were shouting, 'Hosanna to the Son of David! Blessed is the one who comes in the name of the Lord!'
MATTHEW 21:9

Jesus, the donkey-riding Messiah,
you are present with us now,
meeting us through the gospel story.

With the crowds that welcomed you to Jerusalem,
their cloaks laid down and arms raised high,
thrilled by your presence and your claims,
we praise and honour you:
　　Hosanna to the Son of David!
　　Blessed is the one who comes in the name of the Lord!

With the disciples who journeyed with you
and heard all you had to say
of the rejection and suffering that lay ahead,
we praise and honour you:
　　Hosanna to the Son of David!
　　Blessed is the one who comes in the name of the Lord!

With the exploited and downtrodden,
who saw in you the one who was on their side,
overturning the tables of greed and injustice,
we praise and honour you:
　　Hosanna to the Son of David!
　　Blessed is the one who comes in the name of the Lord!

With the wounded ones, the blind and the lame,
who found in you a true welcome and hope
and were touched by your healing grace,
we praise and honour you:
>Hosanna to the Son of David!
>Blessed is the one who comes in the name of the Lord!

With the children whose joy filled the temple
as they cried out in excitement, joy and praise,
scandalising those who would have had you silenced,
we praise and honour you:
>Hosanna to the Son of David!
>Blessed is the one who comes in the name of the Lord!

With your friends and followers of today,
and all who are longing for change to come,
for hope and peace to dawn,
we praise and honour you:
>Hosanna to the Son of David!
>Blessed is the one who comes in the name of the Lord!

30   The son who truly said 'yes'

Matthew 21:18—22:14

**'What do you think? A man had two sons; he went to the first
and said, "Son, go and work in the vineyard today."'**
MATTHEW 21:28

Father in heaven,
you are the mystery beyond our words,
yet we are no mystery to you.

Forgive us, your foolish children,
for words that deny your claim upon our lives,
and far worse, those times when we claim you as our Lord
but fail to truly live out your way
in our attitudes and actions.

Forgive our fixed minds and careless living,
which deny that grace, that truth,
revealed in the works and words
of your dear and loving son, Jesus,
whose 'yes' for you led him
to arrest, mockery and a lonely cross.

31   Questions

Matthew 22:15–46

**One of them, a lawyer, asked him a question to test him.
'Teacher, which commandment in the law is the greatest?'**
MATTHEW 22:35–36

Questions, questions spill around my head:
questions of government and politics,
ethics and morality;
questions of choice and priorities,
knowledge and understanding.
And questions directed at you, my God.
What is it that you wish from me today?
How can I play my part within the life of my nation,
my community and society,
and still stay true to who you call me to be?
What is the living hope I can hold even now?
Amid all that science says about our material world,
how can I say I believe in the resurrection of the dead?
Can these dry bones live?
Does the Sadducees' joke still play true,
heaven overcrowded with past husbands?
I cannot say, but this I know:
you are the living God and the God of the living;
the God of Abraham, Isaac and Jacob;
the God and Father of our Lord Jesus Christ;
my God, my hope, my love.
Stir up your love within me,
my loving God,
love for you and love for neighbour,
near and far.
Questions, questions spill around my head;
your answer is love, made real and true,
spoken and lived out in Jesus.

32   Weightier matters

Matthew 23:1–36

'Woe to you, scribes and Pharisees, hypocrites! For you tithe mint, dill, and cummin, and have neglected the weightier matters of the law: justice and mercy and faith.'
MATTHEW 23:23

Lord Jesus,
how is it that your blessings
have turned to woes, curses and laments?
How is it that you, the humble and gentle one,
who invite us to come and rest,
speak such harsh and bitter words?
It is compassion that enflames you,
justice that fires your soul.
Your anger is pure and unsullied;
anger at those who place burdens
on the shoulders of the weak;
anger at those who lock others
out of your all-embracing kingdom;
anger at those who manipulate
and control the vulnerable,
using others for their own twisted ends;
anger at the outward show of piety,
hiding hypocrisy and greed;
anger at the violence
in the heart of humanity.
Your rage is fearsome,
yet cleansing.
Lord, have mercy.
Touch us with your fire,
but give us your grace too.
Give us your hope,
your peace.

33   The hen and chicks

Matthew 23:37—24:14

'Jerusalem, Jerusalem, the city that kills the prophets and stones those who are sent to it! How often have I desired to gather your children together as a hen gathers her brood under her wings, and you were not willing!'
MATTHEW 23:37

Jesus,
like a mother hen and her brood,
you long to gather your offspring.
In the face of the world's violence and cruelty,
I come under your protective wing.
In the face of my own confusions and fears,
I come under your protective wing.
In the face of every doubt and question,
I come under your protective wing,
to be warmed by your grace,
surrounded by your tenderness.
I come, not to escape the world,
but that I may face it,
with new courage,
truthfulness
and love.

34   The break-in

Matthew 24:15–51

'But understand this: if the owner of the house had known in
what part of the night the thief was coming, he would have
stayed awake and would not have let his house be broken into.
Therefore you also must be ready, for the Son of Man is coming
at an unexpected hour.'

MATTHEW 24:43–44

Our houses are secure
with locks on every window,
doors well bolted with chains just in case
and alarm systems for added protection.
Insurance covers the rest.
Communities become gated and closed.
On our streets CCTV plots every movement
and patrols come when they can.
National security is paramount.
The war on terror continues,
the search for weapons of mass destruction,
clandestine operations against rogue states
and those masked and menacing extremists.
The nuclear deterrent is there
to secure ultimate destruction.

So how will you, the Son of Man,
come to our world today?
How will you enter our protected space
as the beloved at the door,
the light to flood our lives?
It will not be an easy job.
What is your plan in the face of all our defences?

Come, Lord, not as a thief in the night,
but as a welcomed guest.
You are greater than all our possessions,
all our defence systems, all our fears.

Come, Son of Man, Son of God,
true humanity and true divinity,
brought near.
Enter our world this day
and at the end of all days.

35   Where shall we meet you?

Matthew 25:1–46

'Lord, when was it that we saw you hungry or thirsty or a
stranger or naked or sick or in prison, and did not take care
of you?'
MATTHEW 25:44

Where shall we meet you today,
Christ of many disguises?

Will it be only in the victims
who are innocent and helpless,
passive or docile?

Or will we hear you crying out
in those who are furious for justice,
longing for freedom,
desperate for change?

Will we see you only in the little ones of your church,
your faithful or stumbling disciples,
or will we hear your voice
in those of many faiths and none?

Will it be only in the poor that you will come,
or will we touch you in those worn down by their wealth,
bewildered by busyness, confused by consumerism?

And when we meet you,
Christ of many disguises,
give us grace to respond to your need,
not because we have seen you
or recognised you,

but simply because
the need is there
and you have called us
to do what we can.

So replenish the oils of kindness within us,
give us courage to risk ourselves for others
and lighten our lives with your unexpected presence.

36   Made ready

Matthew 26:1–30

Now while Jesus was at Bethany in the house of Simon the leper, a woman came to him with an alabaster jar of very costly ointment, and she poured it on his head as he sat at the table.
MATTHEW 26:6–7

As a table is set
with fresh baked bread
and wine newly poured,
so you, Lord Jesus,
were made ready
by a woman's touch,
fragrant oil
poured over your head.
You are not with us today
in flesh and blood;
we cannot smell you,
but in serving others we can touch you.
We can echo
your extravagant, forgiving love,
poured out like the oil
that dripped down your face;
poured out like the wine you shared
with your followers
and share with us today.
Make us ready, Lord,
for your work today.

37   Going farther

Matthew 26:31–75

And going a little farther, he threw himself on the ground and prayed, 'My Father, if it is possible, let this cup pass from me; yet not what I want but what you want.'
MATTHEW 26:39

God beyond and beside us,
we thank you for Jesus of Nazareth,
our shepherd and our Lord,
who goes ahead of us,
leading the way.

We thank you for his going
into the place of testing,
where prayer is stretched to breaking point
before the cup of suffering,
as he places his life in your hands.

We thank you for his going
into the place of betrayal,
where hatred meets weakness,
fear meets greed,
and his life is sold with a kiss.

We thank you for his going
into the place of denial,
where his disciples run and scatter
and his closest friend turns his back,
swearing he knows nothing,
before those bitter tears flow.

We thank you for his going
into the place of rejection,
where trumped-up charges and expediency
lead on to violence and mockery,
and the demand for his death.

We thank you for his going before us,
through the places of testing and betrayal,
denial and rejection,
to Galilee and beyond,
the place of encounter and new life,
that he promised even in his darkest hour.

38   Blood on our hands

Matthew 27:1–26

Then the people as a whole answered, 'His blood be on us and on our children!'
MATTHEW 27:25

Our hands are not clean,
Lord of the cross.
Jew and Christian, Muslim and Hindu,
agnostic and atheist, religious or non-believer,
we share in this human history of hatred.
No self-righteousness can save us.
No pride or purity of race can help us.
Blood is on our hands.

We have sinned by betraying innocent blood,
once long ago at the Place of the Skull
and again and again in the long story of humanity.

Your blood is on our hands.
No ritual cleaning,
no cleansing agent,
no scientific advance,
no amount of money
can wash it from our hands.

Lord of the cross,
touch our hearts once more,
the hearts of humanity itself.
In your forsakenness, call us back.
Breathe your breath into our lives,
that, with that war-torn soldier who stood at your cross,
we may say,
'Truly you are God's Son.'

39   The Son of God dies

Matthew 27:27-66

Then Jesus cried again with a loud voice and breathed his last.
MATTHEW 27:50

So the Son of God dies,
beaten time after time,
clothed in a clown's crown of twisted thorns
and mocked as a king in a scarlet robe.
The glorious Son of God has carried his cross
and been stripped to bloodied flesh and bone,
wine forced into his face
and jeers from every corner:
'He who saved others cannot save himself.'
He has breathed his last.
The Son of God is dead,
denied, dismissed, deceased.
One more body among so many.
He can cause no more trouble now.
Yet reports of curtains torn,
rocks that move and a centurion's words
hint of more to come.
This Son of God can still move across this earth
and touch hearts and minds
with his pain and his power,
then and now.
Thanks be to God.

40   Shaken by joy

Matthew 28:1–20

Suddenly Jesus met them and said, 'Greetings!' And they came to him, took hold of his feet, and worshipped him.
MATTHEW 28:9

Risen Lord Jesus,
God with us always,
we greet you,
we worship you,
we follow you this day.
You have turned
old fears into new joy,
old doubts into new faith,
defeating ancient death,
finally and forever,
at the beginning of a new glorious day.
Your risen reality touches every place and time.
You have shaken us
into the presence of God,
the kingdom of heaven,
the company of your friends.
Go ahead of us this day:
lead on, Lord of all time,
Lord of all life.
Lead us on, always and forever. Amen.

2

Praying with Mark

As the earliest and shortest of the gospels, Mark's gospel is vivid, stark and fast-paced in its style. Its teaching about prayer is confined to short descriptions of Jesus at prayer and brief sayings about the different dimensions of prayer. There are none of the profound sermon on the mount teachings on prayer found in Matthew's gospel, the striking parables on prayer found in Luke's, or the great prayers of exaltation and intercession found in John's account.

Yet the brevity of Mark's stories and teaching about prayer should not deceive us into thinking that prayer is unimportant in this gospel. In reality, prayer is an underlying current throughout the book, explicitly referred to at crucial moments and implicit time and again. Jesus' teaching on prayer is confined largely to one passage (Mark 11:22–25), but Jesus' example of prayer is seen repeatedly. Mark is very clear that discipleship is about following Jesus and this includes following his way of praying.

For Mark the praying of Jesus is bound up with his relationship to God as child to parent. This is highlighted early on with God's affirmation of Jesus as beloved son and the Spirit's empowerment at Jesus' baptism (Mark 1:9–11). Then the Spirit drives Jesus into the desert, where Jesus wrestles with temptation during an extended time of spiritual struggle. As his ministry unfolds he withdraws to remote places to pray; he heals by authoritative command, touch and words of forgiveness; he grieves at people's hardness of heart; he takes his disciples away to be refreshed; he has compassion on the crowd; he gives thanks for bread and fish, blessing God before sharing them among the crowds; he goes up the mountain to pray; he looks up to heaven and sighs, before giving the word of healing, 'Ephthatha' (Mark 7:34); he blesses children whom the disciples tried to turn away. Having entered Jerusalem to the crowd's acclamation, Jesus confronts the corruption of the temple, using the words of Isaiah, 'My house shall be called a house of prayer' (Mark 11:17); he sums up the commandments in the great *Shema* – 'Hear, O Israel' (Mark 12:29) – linking it to love of neighbour; he gives thanks for bread and wine at the Passover meal, his last supper, and leads his disciples into Gethsemane to pray.

There in the garden Jesus utters his supreme prayer, to Abba, Father, seeking the removal of the cup of suffering that lies ahead of him but then accepting 'not what I want, but what you want' (Mark 14:36). The great Abba prayer of Gethsemane then leads on to the desolation of the cross, where Jesus cries out, using words from the 22nd psalm, 'My God, my God, why have you forsaken me?' (Mark 15:34). This in turn leads on to the affirmation of the centurion, 'Truly this man was God's Son!' (Mark 15:39), and that of the young man at the tomb, 'Do not be alarmed; you are looking for Jesus of Nazareth, who was crucified. He has been raised; he is not here' (Mark 16:6).

In these subtle and varied ways prayer flows through the gospel, and Jesus is presented as the central guide to prayer by his words and example. Mark invites us to pray to God with that intimacy, confidence and intensity that Jesus showed as he prayed 'Abba, Father'. He also challenges us to pray, 'not what I want, but what you want' and to follow the way of self-giving love and service Jesus supremely lived out.

1   Are we ready?

Mark 1:1-13

The beginning of the good news of Jesus Christ, the Son of God.
MARK 1:1

Are we ready in heart and mind and spirit?
Are we ready to hear that wilderness voice, preparing the way,
    calling us to turn round and start again?

Are we ready to welcome the one who is so full of your Spirit,
    so immersed in your love?
Are we ready to join that struggle to overcome all that distorts
    and damages and destroys?
Are we ready for that outburst of your gracious power, that
    Spirit's song, to echo in our hearts and open up our lives?

God of grace, as we journey into this gospel,
this strange good news,
which is life and death and life renewed,
make us ready and willing to hear and to receive,
to turn and to follow,
that we too may be part of your gospel story
now in this time, this moment.

2   Call

Mark 1:14–34

And Jesus said to them, 'Follow me…'
MARK 1:17

Lord Jesus,
friend of fishermen and ordinary folk,
we thank you that you come and interrupt our self-contained lives.
You move us with your call,
challenging us to follow your steps and to join your fishing
    expedition.

Lord Jesus,
friend of all,
we thank you that you come into the midst of life,
the workplace with its demands and compromises,
the place of worship and reflection,
the place of sickness and desperate need,
the place of food shared and friendships deepened.

Lord Jesus,
friend of God,
we thank you that you come and show us the ways of God,
the God who stretches out hands,
in greeting and challenge,
liberating and blessing,
healing and raising to new life.

3   A deserted place

Mark 1:35–45

In the morning, while it was still very dark, he got up and went out to a deserted place, and there he prayed.
MARK 1:35

The dawn is yet to come, the darkness remains,
and, while others sleep,
Jesus slips away to a deserted place.
And I follow at a distance to see what he is about.
There alone in that desert land, he watches and listens:
    the sun is rising yet the air remains cool and crisp;
    the sound of a single bird high in the sky echoes across
       the valley;
    the scent of dew on the stones and shrubs fills the air;
    and now sheer silence, deep and unbroken.
And there I see him pray:
    Jesus stands as the beloved before the love-giver,
    as the child in his parent's arms,
    the chosen one before the one who has chosen;
    now his oneness with the living God is so clear.
The moment is there, hanging in the stillness:
    and now the moment is broken;
    the journey must continue;
    this good news, this deep joy,
    this glorious, reckless love must be shared,
    now and every day.

4 Healing and forgiveness

Mark 2:1–12

Then some people came, bringing to him a paralysed man, carried by four of them.

MARK 2:3

Let us praise God
for friends who stand beside us,
    those who carry us through the darkest of times,
    those who believe in us and for us,
    those who pray for our well-being and bring us to the Lord.
Let us praise God
for the work of healing,
    all who minister to the paralysed:
    surgeons, nurses, doctors and physiotherapists,
    encouraging each tiny step towards recovery,
    psychiatrists, counsellors and listeners,
    helping those traumatised and afraid.
Let us praise God
for words of forgiveness
    that bring hope and healing deep within the human spirit.
Let us praise God
for the authority of Jesus to forgive,
to take from us
    the guilt that paralyses the spirit,
    the fear that hides all hope,
    the isolation that brings despair.
Let us praise God
for the work of healing in body, mind and spirit,
    the work of human kindness and skill,
    the work of divine compassion and grace.

5   From money table to meal table

Mark 2:13–22

'I have come to call not the righteous but sinners.'
MARK 2:17

God of new beginnings and overflowing grace,
we thank you for Levi,
the courageous one,
who steps out of the confines of business and family connections
to follow Jesus with all the challenges that will bring.

We thank you for Levi,
the welcoming one,
who invites his friends to meet the Jesus who has entered his life.

We thank you for Levi,
the dependent one,
who knows that he cannot heal himself,
cannot start again by himself,
cannot forgive himself or find his own way,
but knows that Jesus can do this,
like a good doctor healing a sick patient,
like a bridegroom loving the bride,
like fresh new clothes replacing those that are threadbare,
like new wine bringing joy to heart and soul.

We thank you for Levi,
the glad one,
who rejoices in the call of Jesus
in the best way he or we can,
with a meal for friends, a celebration and a party;
not some stuffy event for the select few,
but open to all who see their need
for that food that Jesus can give.

6 Stretching hands and hearts

Mark 2:23—3:6

He was grieved at their hardness of heart and said to the man, 'Stretch out your hand.'
MARK 3:5

Lord of all my days,
guard my heart from stubbornness and fear.
Let me hear your piercing challenge
to a faith that shrivels, becoming narrow and hard,
like a flower that is closed,
like a bud that will not open.
Let me feel your anger
at those who close their minds
to broken humanity and to your ways.
Let me know your deep distress.
Let me receive your healing,
restoring shrivelled hands and heart to usefulness,
stretching my mind into wonder,
my life into that abundance
you desire for me.

7   Sent out

Mark 3:7–19

**He went up the mountain and called to him those whom he
wanted, and they came to him.**

MARK 3:13

So, Lord, this is what you call the twelve to be:
those that are with you and those that are sent out
to preach and act with your power,
to unify your followers as one new nation.
Lord, forgive your church today
for its failures and foolishness.
When we fail to be with you,
draw us back to yourself.
When we fail to speak or act in your gracious power,
reinvigorate us with your Spirit.
When we forget your commission and become instead a
    cosy club,
send us out once more.

8   Our brother Jesus

Mark 3:20–35

**'Whoever does the will of God is my brother and sister
and mother.'**
MARK 3:35

God who is to us the great Abba,
Father and Mother to all,
we thank you for our dear brother Jesus.
We praise you for your Spirit,
at work so gracefully in him
and touching lives in our day too.
Guard us from all falsehood and distortion.
Keep us from the great sin of seeing good as evil and evil as
    good.
Free us from all that binds us so firmly,
that we may know your will for our lives in the complexity of life
and act on what we know.
Help us to dare to live as your children,
brothers and sisters, parents and children,
within that new reality that Jesus brings,
your kingdom of grace, your circle of love.

9   Seed of grace

Mark 4:1–20

And these are the ones sown on the good soil: they hear the word and accept it and bear fruit, thirty and sixty and a hundredfold.

MARK 4:20

Seed of grace, Word of life
deep within us,
be warmed by the Great Sun;
be watered by the Great Spirit;
be nurtured by the Great Shepherd.

Seed of grace, Word of life,
do not let your hope be taken from us;
do not let our joy in you evaporate;
do not let love for you be choked by self-concern.

Seed of grace, Word of life,
bear a great harvest in hearts open to your goodness,
in lives touched and healed and changed,
multiplying your bounty again and again,
until your kingdom comes.

10   The growing mustard seed

Mark 4:21–34

With what can we compare the kingdom of God, or what parable will we use for it?
MARK 4:30

Mustard-seed God,
you work in hidden ways,
sowing your seed of life
in hearts and minds,
cultures and communities.
We praise you for your hidden ways.
Here are no pyrotechnics, no great trumpet calls,
no visions of blazing light or glorious victories.
Instead you point us to a tiny seed,
hidden and vulnerable,
sown in the muddy soil of life,
growing among us and changing our ways for good,
growing beyond measure and control,
a wondrous tree that gives shade to all parched by the
    world's ways.
We praise you, we thank you for the kingdom seed,
Jesus, who gives life again and again.

11   The storm and the questions

Mark 4:35—5:20

He woke up and rebuked the wind, and said to the sea, 'Peace! Be still!'
MARK 4:39

Our minds, Lord, are full of questions:
    How was the storm stilled?
    What were the spirits that bound Legion?
    Why did the pigs die in such numbers?
    Why did you send the man home?
And questions echo through these stories:
the desperate question of the disciples:
    Teacher, do you not care that we are perishing?
And yours to them – when the wind had been rebuked
and the sea had been told to be still – your questions to us too:
    Why are you afraid?
    Have you still no faith?
Legion's demons recognise and ask:
    What have you to do with me, Jesus, Son of God?
as if claiming that this man is beyond your reach,
outside your territory of care.
But you ask the human question,
the question that recognises the man behind the broken chains,
the bruises, howls and nakedness, the madness and isolation;
you ask:
    What is your name?
And from there you draw this broken man back to his humanity,
to a conversation, sitting together in peace.

From there you draw this rejected scrap of humanity back into
    his community,
encouraging him simply to go back to his friends (he has friends,
    thank God)
and to tell them how much the Lord has done for him
and what mercy he has shown.
Lord Jesus, speak your peace to us.
Still our questions.
Name us and renew our humanity,
that we may proclaim all you have done for us
and that great mercy you have shown us.

12   Hem and hand

Mark 5:21–43

He took her by the hand and said, 'Talitha cum,' which means, 'Little girl, get up!'
MARK 5:41

God of all,
we hold before you
the desperate of our world:
    parents anxious for a sick child,
    torn apart by seeing their son or daughter wracked by pain,
    fearing for the worst,
    people who live day by day with incurable illness.
We hold before you
those who voice their longings in words and prayers,
who look to you for help.
We hold before you
those who can find no words,
yet reach out to you all the same.

Come to their aid, dear Lord.
Give them the faith they need for the hardest days,
that fear may be kept at bay.
Keep their love strong,
    a love for a child that can echo your love,
    a love for life that can echo your love too.
May they know your peace in life, in death and in life restored.
We ask in the name of Jesus, who bled on a cross and whom you
    raised up to life,
turning lament into laughter,
grey bleakness into glorious wonder.
Thanks be to you, eternal God,
for your gift beyond words.

13   Rejection and mission

Mark 6:1–13

He called the twelve and began to send them out two by two, and gave them authority over unclean spirits.
MARK 6:7

In the journey of life,
Lord Jesus,
be a staff to me.
    A staff to lean upon when I am lame,
    struggling to keep walking with you.
    A staff to defend me
    against the dangers around me and within,
    the dark voices that call me to turn back.
    A staff to point out the way ahead,
    to direct and encourage.
    A staff to remind me of Moses and David
    and all who have found hope replacing fear
    and God's comfort on the darkest paths.

In the journey of life,
Lord Jesus,
be a staff to me
and all whom you send out in your name,
to speak in your name,
to stand out against evil,
to share in your healing work,
to pour out your goodness and mercy.

14   Death interrupts

Mark 6:14–29

Immediately the king sent a soldier of the guard with orders to bring John's head. He went and beheaded him in the prison, brought his head on a platter and gave it to the girl...
MARK 6:27–28

A girl dancing.
A drunken promise.
And a man is dead,
his head lying stupidly
on a platter, the final insult.
The bloody suddenness of it
would shock us to the bone,
if we were not so hardened.
Sudden violent deaths are so much
part of our world and our history:
the purges, the gas chambers, the trenches, the killing fields,
the soldier standing on the IED,
the teenager and the lunging knife,
the plunging airplane, the running child and speeding car.

Death interrupts suddenly and fiercely,
leaving tattered pieces in its wake and numbed, grieving hearts.

John's disciples came and took the body,
burying the remains to return some dignity
to the man who had inspired them.
And Herod remained troubled and confused, seeing ghosts,
seeing John in Jesus' work.

Lord, in a world where death can come so viciously,
without rhyme or reason,
give us courage
to hold to faith,
to speak out against evil,
to seek justice,
to make peace,
and to keep hope alive.

15   Green grass

Mark 6:30–44

As he went ashore he saw a great crowd; and he had compassion for them, because they were like sheep without a shepherd...

MARK 6:34

For times of rest and places that refresh
and the one to whom we can open our hearts:
    we thank you, life-giving God.
For the green grass, growing so abundantly
when the rains come and the parched land drinks its fill:
    we thank you, life-giving God.
For the crowds of people, women and men, young and old,
awkward and beautiful, battered and anxious,
each with their gifts and needs:
    we thank you, life-giving God.
For the one who looks at all with compassion,
whose words bring life and whose hands break bread:
    we thank you, life-giving God.
For the gift of bread, offered and blessed,
torn apart and shared among many
to nourish and sustain, bringing strength and joy:
    we thank you, life-giving God.
For nothing wasted, crumbs gathered in a basket
and none left hungry:
    we thank you, life-giving God.
For signs of your overflowing kingdom, glimpses of your
    abundant will,
the taste of your all-embracing banquet:
    we thank you, life-giving God.
So by your Spirit help us to rest and to be fed,
to look at all with compassion and leave none lost or hungry,
for the sake of our great shepherd, Jesus Christ.

16 Passing glory

Mark 6:45–56

'Take heart, it is I; do not be afraid.'
MARK 6:50

We praise you,
God of mountain and mystery,
sea and storm,
presence and peace.

You were there with Moses,
opening up a glimpse of your glory and goodness,
through the cleft of a rock,
merciful and gracious,
abounding in love,
steadfast in faithfulness.

You were there with Elijah,
speaking out in the sound of sheer silence,
a silence that came through the storm and earthquake
and quenched the fire.

You were there in Jesus,
on mountaintop and stormy lake,
there in his words:
'Take heart, it is I; do not be afraid,'
words that calmed the raging wind
and touched hardened hearts.

You are here through the Spirit,
opening up glimpses of glory and goodness,
speaking in the sound of sheer silence,
making yourself known as the one
who can touch hardened hearts.

We praise you,
God of mountain and mystery,
sea and storm,
presence and peace.

17 Lip service

Mark 7:1–23

'This people honours me with their lips, but their hearts are far from me.'
MARK 7:6

When we pay you lip service,
while our hearts are far from you
and our agendas are fixed on ourselves:
    Lord, have mercy.
When we use every trick in the book
to evade our responsibilities
towards those who need us:
    Lord, have mercy.
When we make religion our own
and mould a mirror god
that looks all too familiar:
    Lord, have mercy.
When we focus on the external,
customs or the latest fashion, rituals or appearances,
and forget the need to tend our hearts:
    Lord, have mercy.
When our relationships go wrong,
tainted by greed and delusion,
defiled by pride and folly:
    Lord, have mercy.
Restore us not with whitewash
but from deep within,
for your mercy's sake.

18   Crumbs

Mark 7:24–30

But she answered him, 'Sir, even the dogs under the table eat the children's crumbs.'
MARK 7:28

We come to you, God who has no favourites,
to give thanks for your all-embracing love
for Jew and Gentile, men and women, black and white, straight
    and gay, young and old.

We come to you, God who has no favourites,
to give thanks for your open table,
where none will be treated as dogs,
where all can eat as your beloved children.

We come to you, God who has no favourites,
to give thanks for this story of Jesus and the unnamed woman,
a moment of truth and grace,
for them both and for us all.

We come to you, God who has no favourites,
to ask your help to confront our own prejudices and
    presumptions
and to gain the grace to change our minds and our hearts.

We come to you, God who has no favourites,
to seek that light which is for all nations
and to pray that your salvation may reach to the ends of
    the earth.

19 Be opened

Mark 7:31–37

Then looking up to heaven, he sighed and said to him, 'Ephphatha,' that is, 'Be opened.'
MARK 7:34

Lord Jesus, you have done everything well,
amazing us again and again
with the power and wisdom of your words,
the strength and compassion of your actions,
the depth and intensity of your being.
You have opened our ears
to the truth of God,
not the god of the theorist
or the totem of the religious,
but the living God who is the source of true life.
You have opened our eyes
to see the world, the world in the light of love,
not as a means to an end
or an object to be used,
but as a treasure of great wonder, a place of great need.
You have opened our tongues
to sing in praise and to speak humbly of your grace.
Lord Jesus, you have done everything well:
accept our thanks and praise, our wonder and joy,
this and every day.

20   Sign and no sign

Mark 8:1–21

... and he took the seven loaves, and after giving thanks he broke them and gave them to his disciples to distribute...
MARK 8:6

Like the Pharisees, we demand signs, dear Lord:
signs that you are real and at work among us,
signs that you care and hear our prayers.
Yet you sigh and tell us:
no sign will be given,
no knock-out proof that you are with us and at work.
Instead you take bread and give thanks,
blessing your God and ours.
You give and call your friends to help in the giving.
And as we are fed,
and as we find that many others are fed too,
thousands upon thousands,
our hearts are softened,
our eyes are cleared,
and our ears are opened.
We remember how in every generation you have done this,
feeding so many that we could never count them,
calling so many to share in the task of feeding your world.
Keep us from failing to see or understand.
Keep us from hardening our hearts or closing our ears.
Speak your word of thanks, your word of compassion.

21 Partial vision

Mark 8:22—9:1

'For those who want to save their life will lose it, and those who lose their life for my sake, and for the sake of the gospel, will save it.'
MARK 8:35

God of perfect vision,
we see, yet we do not see;
    a mist covers our hearts,
    a self-concern distorts our vision,
    a lack of imagination narrows our view of the world.
We beg for your touch
to liberate us from our blindness
that we may see Jesus,
    the promised Messiah,
    the man of the cross,
    the one who loses his life to save ours.
We beg for your touch again to clear our vision
that we may see people not as objects – trees in the way –
but truly as your children, unique, vulnerable, dear to you.
We beg for your touch again,
that we may not only see, but that we may also follow,
    forgetting ourselves,
    losing ourselves,
    giving ourselves,
    in the tasks you have for us this day.

22   Glimpse of glory

Mark 9:2-13

Six days later, Jesus took with him Peter and James and John, and led them up a high mountain apart, by themselves.
MARK 9:2

Lead us to the mountain, great God,
the majestic mountain that shows us our smallness,
raising our spirits and enlarging our minds.

Lead us to the light, great God,
the dazzling light that reveals the goodness of Jesus,
piercing the darkness of our doubts and fears.

Lead us to the vision, great God,
the glorious vision of the lawgiver, the prophet and the Son,
bound together in love for you and the world.

Lead us to the mystery, great God,
the cloud of unknowing, the shadow of your being,
stretching over us, like a tender hand.

Lead us to that point, great God,
where we can truly listen,
truly hear the word of Christ
for our world at this moment.

Lead us down the mountain, great God,
to the place of service,
the place where faith must work,
hope must be held, love must be shared.

23   I believe, help my unbelief

Mark 9:14–29

Immediately the father of the child cried out, 'I believe; help my unbelief!'
MARK 9:24

God of powerful vulnerability,
we thank you for the praying of Jesus,
filling his encounter with a heart-torn parent and a broken boy
with resurrection power.
We hold before you all whom the church has failed,
by weakness of prayer or the abuse of power,
by the failure to listen or the unwillingness to become involved,
by lack of imagination or narrowness of minds.
Too many cries have gone unheard.
Too many children have lives that are bound or broken.

God of powerful vulnerability,
renew your people in this time of bewildering change.
Cast out our fear and faithlessness.
Bring us to our knees, that with a desperate father
of another age, we too may cry,
'We believe; help our unbelief!'
And, like the boy, may we be raised to our feet,
to share in your work of powerful vulnerability.

24   The greatest

Mark 9:30–50

**But they were silent, for on the way they had argued with one
another who was the greatest.**
MARK 9:34

Confront us, dear Lord,
with all that holds us back
from following your way of grace and peace.
Confront us with our lack of understanding
of your costly cross and suffering love,
victorious over death itself.
Confront us with our false priorities and distorted comparisons,
our arguments over who is greater.
Confront us with our unwillingness to see the good others do,
the generous acts by people who are different from ourselves.
Confront us with all that makes us stumble,
all that builds a false kingdom, not of your making.

Show us again your cross and empty tomb,
your joyful presence among us,
there to bring life abundantly.

Show us the child, any child,
your representative here on earth,
there to be welcomed joyfully.

Show us the cup of water,
there to be given generously
and received thankfully.

25 The welcoming one

Mark 10:1–16

**'Truly I tell you, whoever does not receive the kingdom of God
as a little child will never enter it.'**
MARK 10:15

Blessed be our God,
the Creator who formed humanity,
male and female in the divine image.

Blessed be our God,
the Saviour who welcomes each child
and enfolds humanity in the divine blessing.

Blessed be our God,
the Spirit who draws humanity together,
joining those once separate in the divine community.

Blessed be our God,
the Trinity – Creator, Saviour and Spirit –
there at the beginning of all things,
there at the heart of all life,
there at the fulfilment of the divine kingdom.

26   How shall I respond?

Mark 10:17–31

Jesus, looking at him, loved him and said, 'You lack one thing…'
MARK 10:21

How shall I respond
   to your invitation
     to look again at life?
How shall I respond
   to your call
     to live the right way?
How shall I respond
   to your look
     of love for me?
How shall I respond
   to your challenge
     to let go of those things that possess me?
How shall I respond
   to your demand
     to reach out to the poor?
How shall I respond
   to your beckoning to follow you,
     here and now, whatever my life may be?
How shall I respond
   to my freedom
     to walk with you or to turn back?
How shall I respond?

27   Servant

Mark 10:32–45

'But it is not so among you; but whoever wishes to become great among you must be your servant.'
MARK 10:43

Where we use our faith for our own selfish ends,
seeking the best seats in heaven,

 Lord Jesus, speak your word of authority:

 'It shall not be so among you.'

Where we play the power game, making comparisons with
 others,

sensing our own superiority, grasping at status,

 Lord Jesus, speak your word of authority:

 'It shall not be so among you.'

Where we build hierarchies, looking for others to lead and direct,
forgetting the way of service,

 Lord Jesus, speak your word of authority:

 'It shall not be so among you.'

Where we forget the cost of discipleship,

the letting go of baptism, the drinking of the cup, the way of
 the cross,

 Lord Jesus, speak your word of authority:

 'It shall not be so among you.'

Lord Jesus, show us the servant way.

Renew your church

to be a people where there is no lording over others,

no 'us' and 'them',

no best and worst seats,

but one body

baptised in you, fed by you,

sharing your cup of blessing with the world.

28   Blessed is the one

Mark 10:46—11:11

[They shouted:] 'Hosanna! Blessed is the one who comes in the name of the Lord!'
MARK 11:9

Jesus, friend of blind beggars,
we rejoice in your coming
and offer you our cries for help and our shouts of triumph.
With your fallible followers of every age,
we pray, 'Have mercy,'
and sing, 'Hosanna! Hosanna in highest heaven!'
You ride a young donkey,
mocking our delusions of grandeur and grasps for power.
You are no ordinary king:
no King David, using power for selfish ends;
no King Herod, mixing weakness with tyranny;
no Caesar, with worldly empire grounded in violence.
You do not lord it over your subjects,
but come in humble life-giving glory.
Your kingdom breaks into our world and into our lives,
as vision is restored, hope is made real, joy bursts out,
peace is given a chance.

Hosanna! Blessed are you, Lord Jesus.
Blessed is your kingdom!
Blessed is the promise you bring to our troubled world.
Hosanna in highest heaven!

29 House of prayer

Mark 11:12–25

He was teaching and saying, 'Is it not written, "My house shall be called a house of prayer for all the nations"? But you have made it a den of robbers.'
MARK 11:17

Build a house of prayer, Lord Jesus,
a home not of stones or sacred places,
but made of your people,
your followers of every time and place.

Build a house of prayer, Lord Jesus,
and make me a living stone
within that temple,
centred and dependent on others and on you.

Build a house of prayer, Lord Jesus,
open to all nations, all peoples, all faiths and none,
all seekers after truth and life.

Build a house of prayer, Lord Jesus,
free from corruption or hypocrisy, hatred or fear,
renewed each moment by your Spirit.

Build a house of prayer, Lord Jesus,
a mighty tree that bears fruit in every season,
in faith and forgiveness,
in word and deed.

30   Tenants

Mark 11:27—12:12

'A man planted a vineyard... then he leased it to tenants...'
MARK 12:1

Remind us, God of the beloved,
that we are only tenants, not the owners.
  Not the owners of our children,
    for they must grow to become themselves.
  Not the owners of our homes,
    for they must be places of welcome and friendship.
  Not the owners of the church,
    for the church must be yours, called to your work.
  Not the owners of our nation,
    for there is but one humanity, and we are part of
      each other.
  Not the owners of this planet,
    for earth is your place, created for all your creatures.
Challenge our attempts to seize control,
to satisfy our selfish greed,
to grasp what we consider our inheritance.

Make us willing to receive your prophets of today,
uncomfortable, unexpected voices
that remind us that all is on loan
and all is to be respected.

And show us your beloved Son,
who does not grasp his inheritance,
but offers his life for friend and enemy alike,
for the sake of the vineyard, the earth, the kingdom.

31 Death and taxes

Mark 12:13–27

Jesus said to them, 'Is not this the reason you are wrong, that you know neither the scriptures nor the power of God?'
MARK 12:24

God of demanding justice,
we hold before you the emperors of our day,
    those who hold the power of government:
    those authorised by the vote of the people
    and those who have grasped power by violence or corruption;
    those who exercise influence with wisdom and compassion
    and those whose tyranny is cruel and self-serving.
They have their time,
but YOUR TIME will come.
Confront them with your judgement and mercy.
Expose the wrong and reveal your piercing truth and
    self-giving way.

God of overflowing life,
we hold before you all who have died:
    those who trusted you to the end;
    those who were bewildered and afraid;
    those who cursed you and the night;
    those who hoped for nothing.
They had their time,
but YOUR TIME is greater.
You are the Lord of life,
the God of the living.

Look with mercy on all your creation, all your children.
With Abraham and Isaac and Jacob,
with Moses and Miriam and Elijah,
with Mary and Peter and Mark,
bring us to the glory of your presence,
where, like angels, all sound out your praise,
in joy and gladness, light and peace,
through Jesus Christ, the mighty Saviour and risen Lord.

32   The good scribe

Mark 12:28–44

**When Jesus saw that he answered wisely, he said to him,
'You are not far from the kingdom of God.'**
MARK 12:34

May we learn, Lord Jesus,
from the good scribe,
who echoes your words
and sees how love for God
and neighbour outweigh
all ritual and sacrifices:
    deepen our love.

May we learn, Lord,
from the crowd
who delights to listen to you,
as you put King David in his place
and show yourself as the surprising Messiah:
    open our hearts.

May we learn, Lord,
from the corrupted scribes,
whose lives are all show with no substance,
exposed by you
for their longing for respect,
their disregard for the needy,
their long prayers that do not connect
with God or with life:
    guard us from evil.

May we learn, Lord,
from the widow
whose two small coins speak of sacrifice and grace
and point to your self-giving love
offered on a cross:
    show us your way.

33   Alert and awake

Mark 13:1–37

'And what I say to you I say to all: Keep awake.'
MARK 13:37

We are anxious, Lord of our times,
anxious for ourselves, our children and our children's children.
There are such fearsome signs of disturbance
in the life of humanity and of the planet itself:
nations torn apart by ethnic and religious hatred,
the bitter scars of outrage followed by outrage;
the divide of rich and poor
becoming an unbridgeable chasm,
a deep injustice set to explode.
We are anxious about a faith on the defensive,
facing deadly persecution in so many nations
and mockery in our own.
We worry for the planet's sake,
groaning under the heat of our consumption
and the weight of our numbers.
False prophets come proclaiming your greatness, yet living a lie.
Would-be messiahs peddle beguiling answers
that do not match reality.
Fear gathers yet more fear.
Where are we to turn?

Come, Holy Spirit,
give us new words to speak,
to bring hope to your world.
Come, Holy Spirit,
wake us up to the cries of our planet.

Come, Holy Spirit,
make us watchful for signs of the kingdom,
breaking into the life of this world.
Come, Holy Spirit,
open our ears to the words of Christ,
the words that will never pass away.
Come, Holy Spirit,
give us the wisdom to discern uncomfortable truths
and to turn from all that is false.

34 Remember her

Mark 14:1–11

'Truly I tell you, wherever the good news is proclaimed in the whole world, what she has done will be told in remembrance of her.'
MARK 14:9

So it begins:
the plot, the planned arrest under cover of darkness,
the scheme to silence this Jesus.
Money passes hands,
and one who listened to his words and shared his food,
one who walked the dusty roads of Palestine in his company,
one whom he loves
seeks now to betray him.

And in the midst of this darkness
enters an unnamed woman,
a jar of precious perfume,
an action that speaks of a Messiah
and a burial.

God in whose image we are made, female and male,
may this woman remind us of
all women who give costly service,
all women who experience the anger of angry men,
all women who are noticed and affirmed by Jesus,
all women who are caught up in the plots of the powerful,
all women who play their part in your good news story,
your overwhelming, costly, gracious act of love.

35   New in the kingdom of God

Mark 14:12–25

**'Truly I tell you, I will never again drink of the fruit of the vine
until that day when I drink it new in the kingdom of God.'**
MARK 14:25

God beyond time, beyond space,
we thank you for that moment in history,
in a room hidden in Jerusalem,
when Jesus took the bread that friends had prepared.

We thank you for the hands,
tense with all that was to come,
lifting the bread, holding it there before them.

We thank you for the words he spoke,
forgetting the betrayal around him,
focusing all his soul in blessing you,
thanking you for all you gave and give.

We thank you for the breaking,
hands tearing the loaf apart,
crumbs flying, eyes watching,
caught up in the drama of pain and sacrifice.

We thank you for the giving
to each of those frail disciples;
the insistent words he used:
'Take it, this is my body.'

We thank you for the cup,
the words of thanks again,
the offering for all,
his blood poured out not for a few but for many,
the taste of the kingdom to come.

We thank you for that fleeting moment
grounded in time,
held in the confines of a crowded room,
yet resounding down the centuries to touch our lives today,
to feed and refresh us,
to show us your kingdom.

Help us to take what Christ has given,
to bless and thank you,
as he did so long ago.

36   The cup

Mark 14:26–52

'Abba, Father, for you all things are possible; remove this cup from me; yet, not what I want, but what you want.'
MARK 14:36

The cup is there before us,
the mocking cup,
full of the dregs of human suffering,
full of the bitter cruelty,
full of the cheap injustice,
full of the sad sin of the world.

The cup is there and none will drink it.
None place their lips on its deadly rim.

We close our eyes;
we look away;
we pray to the God who seems silent.

And one walks forward
alone
and takes the cup
alone
and hesitates
alone.
'Abba, remove this cup from me,'
he prays
alone.
'Yet not what I want,
but what you want.'
Alone
he prays to the God who seems silent.

And slowly, painfully,
he takes the cup
and drains it to its very depths,
alone,
risking his all for this world,
loving his all for our sakes,
placing his all in the hands
of the God who seems silent.

37   Peter's tears

Mark 14:53-72

Then Peter remembered that Jesus had said to him, 'Before the cock crows twice, you will deny me three times.' And he broke down and wept.

MARK 14:72

Here is Peter's prayer:
not the following at a safe distance,
watching from the sidelines
the death trap closing on Jesus;
not the hasty words of denial,
the pretence of innocence,
the curses and the oaths –
'I do not know this man.'

Here is Peter's prayer:
the sound of dawn
breaking into his mind,
making him remember
the words of his Lord and Teacher, the Galilean Jesus,
the breaking down and flowing tears.

There is Peter's prayer – in tears and brokenness.
So, dear God, we hold before you all who shed bitter tears today:
tears over relationships destroyed, trust broken, faith denied.
May their hot and bitter tears be for you a prayer of brokenness,
that healing and forgiveness may flow once more
and new beginnings come where all was lost.
We ask in the name of our Lord and teacher, the Galilean Jesus.

38   Handed over

Mark 15:1–20

They bound Jesus, led him away, and handed him over to Pilate.
MARK 15:1

We stand in solidarity with all who have been handed over:
handed over to be tried unjustly, tortured and mocked;
handed over to be done to,
dehumanised,
stripped and beaten
reduced to mere flesh.
   May their cries be heard in the corners of heaven.
We stand in solidarity with all who have been handed over
to the will of the mob,
the whim of the powerful,
the plotting of those who know best.
   May their cries shake our world into newness.
We stand in solidarity with Jesus, the thorn-crowned king,
as he stands before Pilate, the emperor's representative,
and amazes him with his stunning silence,
as he absorbs the chief priests' hatred
and satisfies the bloodlust of the crowd,
as he wears the mocking cloak
and receives the lashes, spit and laughter.
   May his cry bring us all to our senses.
We kneel in homage to our thorn-crowned king,
not in mockery, please God,
but in awe and wonder, grief and hope,
determination to rid the world
of the torturers' tools and the powers that bind and destroy
and to follow this Jesus wherever he leads.

39   The body broken and curtain torn

Mark 15:21–47

**Then Jesus gave a loud cry and breathed his last. And the
curtain of the temple was torn in two, from top to bottom.**
MARK 15:37–38

Let us be still before the cross,
not in the company of the mockers –
the passers-by who wag their heads and shout their jeers;
the scribes and chief priests whose mocking cry
rings down the centuries,
'He saved others; he cannot save himself';
the bandits who taunt and jeer in their pain;
and all who look for a sign,
a magic miracle, where Jesus jumps down from the cross
or is helped down by Elijah and all is right with the world.

Let us be still before the cross,
in the company of the women
who followed this carpenter of Nazareth and listened to his words;
the centurion who reported the death and saw the truth;
and that other Joseph who, waiting and longing for your kingdom,
provided a final dignity to that death-torn body.

Let us be still before the cross
and enter its mystery
in the company of the God of Jesus,
who seemed so far off, so absent,
and yet was there in the parting cry,
the final breath, the torn curtain,
death turned into release (for many),
pain become a prayer (for the world),
hatred met by love (for all).

40   He is not here, he is going ahead

Mark 16:1–8

'But go, tell his disciples and Peter that he is going ahead of you to Galilee; there you will see him, just as he told you.'
MARK 16:7

Risen Jesus,
you stun me with your absence.
You cannot be entombed
in rock or stone,
in ecclesiastical structures
or scholarly debates,
scientific definition
or doctrinal niceties.

You cannot be bound
by Satan's powers
or human evils.

You are the strong one,
who turns the tables
on death itself and all wickedness.

I have followed you though these gospel's pages,
but you are not trapped within its words.
You walk free,
beyond its letters,
beyond its control.
You are not in this book,
but let loose
on an unsuspecting world.
You are no tame lion.

You cannot be grasped or controlled,
only followed,
met in the Galilees of the workers and the wounded,
the frail and the fallible;
met among the ordinary
children, women and men;
met in the towns and cities,
hills and valleys of the here and now.

Glory to you, dear Teacher.
Glory to you, the Servant One.
Glory to you, my risen Lord,
here and now and forever. Amen.

3

Praying with Luke

Luke wants his reader – Theophilus (literally, 'friend of God') – to truly know what Jesus did and taught in his earthly ministry (Luke 1:4) and continues to do and teach through his disciples, empowered and sent out into the world by the Holy Spirit (Acts 1:1).

In gathering materials for his 'orderly narrative' it is likely that Luke used Mark's gospel, material also used by Matthew, and sources and traditions uniquely his own. He worked carefully with these materials, respecting their witness, but willing at times to adapt and rearrange them to present his vision of the new dawn brought about by the event of Jesus. Convinced of the necessity and power of prayer, Luke gives special emphasis to praise and prayer within his gospel and continues this theme in his second book, Acts.

He invites us to watch Jesus as he prays, to listen to his stories, to identify with the pleas and prayers of characters within the narrative and to ask for that same gift of God – the Holy Spirit – that filled Jesus and was poured into his followers after his ascension.

Jesus regularly withdraws to remote areas to pray (Luke 5:16). It is on one such occasion, when Jesus 'was praying in a certain place', that one of the disciples asks him, 'Lord, teach us to pray' (Luke 11:1), and Jesus responds by teaching them to say a version of what we now call the Lord's Prayer. For Luke, Jesus is the great teacher of prayer, instructing his disciples by word and example. As well as the teaching included in Mark and Matthew's gospels, there are parables about prayer unique to Luke, in particular the friend asking for loaves (Luke 11:5-8), the widow asking for justice (Luke 18:1-8) and the Pharisee and the tax collector (Luke 18:9-14).

Another of Jesus' parables unique to Luke's telling of the gospel is the parable of the two sons and the loving father. This gives a vivid picture of prayer as the restoration of relationship. Here in this glorious story we see the younger son coming to his senses – 'he came to himself' (Luke 15:17) – recognising his need and returning home, with the loving father running out to meet and embrace him. Then the same father goes out to invite the angry and embittered older son to come and share the celebration, with those compassionate words, 'Son, you are always with me, and all that is mine is yours' (Luke 15:31). To pray with this story is to come close to the God who is reaching out to embrace you, day by day. It also commits us to seek to restore relationships between people.

It is clear that Luke sees prayer as both deeply personal and shared with the community of faith. He describes how the early Christian community followed Jesus' example by giving prayer priority and gathering frequently to pray together. He ends his gospel with the disciples continually in the temple praising God (Luke 24:52) and begins his second book with the disciples in the upper room praying together (Acts 1:14). This vivid picture of people praying, of Jesus' challenge to all to be awake and alert to God in their lives, can inspire us in very different times to seek the same gift of the Spirit to pray with and in us.

1   Your prayer has been heard

Luke 1:1-17

But the angel said to him, 'Do not be afraid, Zechariah, for your prayer has been heard. Your wife Elizabeth will bear a son, and you will name him John.'
LUKE 1:13

Lord God,
    God of Abraham and Sarah,
    God of Hannah and Elkanah,
    God of Ruth and Boaz,
    God of Zechariah and Elizabeth,
we thank you for hearing the cries of your people,
the little desperate prayers offered to you
in the darkness of the night.
We thank you for weaving those cries
into your greater purpose of love,
your work of healing and saving, guiding and renewing.
Hear our little stumbling prayers
and work them into your tapestry of grace and hope.
Uphold us in the waiting times,
the desperate times, the hopeless times.
By your Spirit renew our trust in your greater love,
in Jesus' name.

2 Standing in the presence of God

Luke 1:18–25

The angel replied: 'I am Gabriel. I stand in the presence of God, and I have been sent to speak to you and to bring you this good news.'
LUKE 1:19

We stand in your presence, awesome God.
We are silenced:
    our minds cannot grasp your greatness;
    our hearts remain unsure, unknowing,
    our lives untouched, resistant to your Spirit.
We are silenced.
Forgive us
    our faithless fear,
    our timid response,
    our tiresome questions.
Hold us in the silence,
the stillness, the surrendering,
enough to know
that we stand in your presence,
awesome, forgiving God.

3   Yes to God

Luke 1:26–38

Then Mary said, 'Here am I, the servant of the Lord; let it be with me according to your word.'
LUKE 1:38

Guard us, good Lord,
from the easy yes,
the glib promises of faithfulness,
the familiar phrases of religion.
Confront us with your world-turning reality,
your hopes and dreams for our lives.
Help us through the struggles of faith,
that your promises may be known in us
and that we may truly, honestly answer
that we are your servants,
seeking your kingdom,
willing your will
to be done in us
and our world.

4 Mary's song: love's laughter

Luke 1:39–56

'My spirit rejoices in God my Saviour.'
LUKE 1:47

Great, great God,
laughter swells within me.
Joy and wonder overflow.
You are at work,
even in this –
a child growing like countless others before and since.
You are at work,
to save, to bless, to rescue.
Your love is so tender and so strong,
holy, holy God.
You are at work,
glorious and majestic, deep and awesome.
The proud and mighty are shown their places.
The rich and self-satisfied are shown their emptiness.
The poor and hungry are welcomed
and fed not with scraps but with the finest food.
The little people are lifted high.
You are at work,
in the story of Israel, Abraham and Sarah and all their offspring,
in the story of this child, Jesus, and all who act on his word.
You are at work.

5   A new name and a new dawn

Luke 1:57–80

'By the tender mercy of our God, the dawn from on high will break upon us, to give light to those who sit in darkness and in the shadow of death, to guide our feet into the way of peace.'
LUKE 1:78–79

Jesus, in your conception through the Spirit's power
and Mary's humble obedience,
    the dawn has come, to bring light and peace.
In your birth in poverty, with nothing but love,
    the dawn has come, to bring light and peace.
In your childhood with its hiddenness, growth and grace,
    the dawn has come, to bring light and peace.
In your baptism, opening heaven itself
with the lover's joy in the beloved,
    the dawn has come, to bring light and peace.
In your struggle with the evil one
and your rejection of the easy way,
    the dawn has come, to bring light and peace.
In your proclamation of good news to the poor
and release to the captives,
    the dawn has come, to bring light and peace.
In your calling of the disciples to follow you and not to be afraid,
    the dawn has come, to bring light and peace.
In your healing of the sick and compassion for the outcast,
    the dawn has come, to bring light and peace.
In your love for your enemies and prayers for the wicked,
    the dawn has come, to bring light and peace.
In your acceptance of a woman's kiss and tears
and the forgiveness you gave,
    the dawn has come, to bring light and peace.

In your prayer through the night
and your dazzling brightness on the mountaintop,
  the dawn has come, to bring light and peace.
In your weeping over Jerusalem and entry as king of peace,
  the dawn has come, to bring light and peace.
In your prayer that God's will might be done
and your arrest for our sake,
  the dawn has come, to bring light and peace.
In your look of compassion at Peter who denied knowing you,
  the dawn has come, to bring light and peace.
In your naked love upon a cross,
  the dawn has come, to bring light and peace.
In your death, when the sun's light failed,
  the dawn has come, to bring light and peace.
In your burial in the rock-hewn tomb, witnessed by the women,
  the dawn has come, to bring light and peace.
In your resting on the sabbath in the mystery of death,
  the dawn has come, to bring light and peace.
In your glorious rising again, as living Lord,
  the dawn has come, to bring light and peace.
In your walking with the disciples on the road,
making their hearts burn within them,
  the dawn has come, to bring light and peace.
In your breaking of bread to open their eyes to your presence,
  the dawn has come, to bring light and peace.
In your promise of the Spirit's liberating power,
  the dawn has come, to bring light and peace.
In your blessing from heaven, bringing great joy and worship,
  the dawn has come, to bring light and peace.
Blessed be your name, Lord Jesus Christ, now and forever.

6   No room?

Luke 2:1–7

She gave birth to her firstborn son and wrapped him in bands of cloth, and laid him in a manger, because there was no place for them in the inn.

LUKE 2:7

There is a place for you in the story of an empire that would fall,
a so-called Roman peace that would fail.
There is a place for you in the world of politics and taxes,
a census and bureaucracy, edicts and laws.
There is a place for you in the family history of King David,
the hopes and longings of a faith and a nation.
There is a place for you under the protection of Mary and Joseph,
who in their poverty held you in their care.
There is a place for you among the straw and animals
    of Bethlehem,
a feeding trough of hay made into your crib.
There is a place for you among the towns and cities of our times,
the poverty and squalor, the travel and the trading.
There is a place for you, Jesus, child of Bethlehem,
in our stories and our lives today.
There is a place for you,
this and every day.

7   Glory to God

Luke 2:8-20

'Glory to God in the highest heaven, and on earth peace among those whom he favours!'
LUKE 2:14

> With the angels and shepherds we give our praise:
> Glory to you, God of heaven and earth.

We have heard your voice, in the story of the child born in poverty, bringing delight to Mary and Joseph, joy to the shepherds and the ordinary people, hope to the world:

> With the angels and shepherds we give our praise:
> Glory to you, God of heaven and earth.

We have seen your presence in Jesus, the servant Lord, so close to your heart, opening your grace, your forgiveness, your life to us:

> With the angels and shepherds we give our praise:
> Glory to you, God of heaven and earth.

We have felt your touch in these treasures of faith, these saving stones from the past, these powerful pointers to your Spirit's work here and now, these sure signs of hope for the future:

> With the angels and shepherds we give our praise:
> Glory to you, God of heaven and earth.

We have received your challenge to seek your presence in the ordinary places of life, to accept your shocking grace, and to share your good news with a needy world:

With the angels and shepherds we give our praise:
Glory to you, God of heaven and earth.

We have glimpsed your vision for the world, of conflict ended, justice restored, relationships mended and fear destroyed, and we will walk your way of peace:

With the angels and shepherds we give our praise:
Glory to you, God of heaven and earth.

8 Seeing salvation

Luke 2:21–40

'For my eyes have seen your salvation, which you have prepared in the presence of all peoples.'
LUKE 2:30–31

Here is the peace of God,
the Word of grace and truth made flesh and blood
and held in an old man's arms.

Here is the light to the Gentiles,
not in the power of empire
or the wealth of nations
but in a screaming child
held in an old man's arms.

Here is the glory of Israel,
not in a nation conquering the world in God's name
or a land purified of all foreign presence,
but in a quietened child,
held in an old man's arms.

It is enough to see that child,
to feel the touch of his fingers,
the warmth of his body,
the breeze of his breath.

It is enough to sense the hope
and the pain, the piercing challenge
and the glorious blessing.

It is enough to know the difficult peace
this child brings to this broken world.

Glory to God, in the name of Jesus,
Saviour, Light and Peace.

9   Heaven breaks open

Luke 3:1–38

… when Jesus also had been baptised and was praying, the heaven was opened.

LUKE 3:21

Heaven breaks open,
    for you, Lord Jesus, enter the depths of human life.
Heaven breaks open,
    for you, Lord Jesus, pray from the centre of your soul.
Heaven breaks open,
    for you, Lord Jesus, receive the Spirit's gentle power.
Heaven breaks open,
    for you, Lord Jesus, know the wonder of God's love
        and blessing.
Heaven breaks open,
    for you, Lord Jesus, bring joy and delight to the one who
        sent you.
Heaven breaks open,
    for you, Lord Jesus, call us to share your life today:
    to reach out to everyday people,
    to pray from the centre of our souls,
    to receive your Spirit,
    to know the wonder of God's love,
    and so to bring joy in heaven, peace on earth and glory to
        God's name.
Heaven breaks open.
    Lord Jesus, break open our hearts and minds, by the
        Spirit's flight,
    and raise us up to live your way.

10   Testing to the limit

Luke 4:1–13

Jesus, full of the Holy Spirit, returned from the Jordan and was led by the Spirit in the wilderness.
LUKE 4:1

Uncomfortable God,
guard us from treating you as a soft blanket, a reassuring stick,
a puppet of our own making;
pour out your untamed Spirit into our hearts and minds
      and bodies
to fill us with your life,
to lead us out into the wilderness,
to silence our inner chatter,
to confront us with what is real – good and evil.

Uncomfortable God,
guard us from temptation;
forgive us when we feed our bodies and forget our souls;
forgive us when we look to our own glory and fail to worship you;
forgive us when we test you rather than trust your faithful
      presence.

Uncomfortable God,
turn us to Christ, the disturbing Saviour,
who faced the full force of temptation
and the evil one himself in the silence of the desert
and held on to you, the Lord, the God of all.

11   God's today

Luke 4:14–44

Then he began to say to them, 'Today this scripture has been fulfilled in your hearing.'
LUKE 4:21

I will celebrate this day
the God who speaks and speaks
and speaks again.

I will give thanks for the prophets of the past,
the Isaiahs of ancient times,
whose words still burn in hearts today,
words of liberation for the oppressed,
good news for the poor,
freedom for captives,
sight for all blinded by fear.

I will give thanks for the carpenter's son,
who took old words and made them present,
living them in all he said and did,
breaking the confines of sacred space,
opening life to those long despised and rejected,
disturbing hardened minds and stifled hearts.

I will give thanks for the friend of God's friend,
gathering those words for his own moment of now,
his own people with all they faced,
making the words of Jesus live again.

And I will give thanks for these words
read and spoken again
in my time, my place, my world.

Miracle of miracles,
the Word lives again,
   liberating,
   disturbing,
   opening up life;
the word of Isaiah,
the word of Jesus,
the word of Luke,
the living word of the living God,
who speaks and speaks
and speaks again.

12 Caught in God's net

Luke 5:1—6:49

**'Why do you call me "Lord, Lord", and do not do what
I tell you?'**
LUKE 6:46

Lord Jesus, your words burn in our minds and souls,
and like Peter we are afraid,
fearful of the change you will bring to our lives
this and every day.
Speak your word of grace to us once more,
calling us so powerfully to banish our fears,
to come to you, to hear your word,
to act on all you say.

Lord, have mercy and make us merciful.
Lord, show forgiveness and help us to forgive.
Lord, reveal your kindness and make us kinder.
Stretch our love by your love.
Stretch it to those we so easily judge and condemn.
Stretch it to those we loathe or fear.
Stretch it to those we pass by or ignore.

By your Spirit turn us into better trees,
transform our thorns and brambles into fruiting branches,
and make our hearts abundant, generous and useful,
good soil in which your kingdom seed may grow
and bear good fruit for our wounded world.

13   Only speak the word, Lord

Luke 7:1–10

A centurion there had a slave whom he valued highly, and who was ill and close to death.

LUKE 7:2

Authority frightens us.
Our minds are tainted with all we see of power's corruption,
words used so easily
promises made so lightly.
When it comes to the moment of decision,
that step of utter foolish faith,
we hold back.
We hold on to our need to control the outcome,
to be sure that we will not be fooled.

Jesus, remind us of the centurion,
who amazed you with his faith,
who refused to trouble you,
refused to receive you in his home,
refused to meet you face to face,
yet recognised in you one under divine authority
and made that step of total trust:
'Only speak the word, and let my servant be healed.'

True and gracious Lord,
by your liberating word
enable us to let go of our pride, our fear, our distrust,
that we ourselves may be healed,
made whole by your command.

14   A woman's love for Jesus

Luke 7:36–50

'… hence she has shown great love…'
LUKE 7:47

Foolish Lord,
who came to be hung on a tree and gave me new life and freedom,
accept my love poured out at your feet;
accept the fragrance of my gifts,
money spent extravagantly for you;
accept my tears, streaming wantonly, wetting your toes;
accept my hair as a towel to dry your skin;
accept my kisses, not face to face,
but from the dusty ground of my being.

Foolish Lord,
close your ears to the murmuring voices around me,
telling you that I am dirt, a slut, a non-person,
that kind of woman who should be thrown back into the gutter;
close your eyes to looks of anger and embarrassment;
close your heart to the hurt they intend to inflict on you.

Foolish Lord,
thank you for your joy in my tears and the washing of your feet,
your joy in my constant kisses and perfumed oil;
thank you for revealing the love within me
and the forgiveness I have received.

Foolish Lord,
send me out in faith, saved by you, to live your peace,
and help me to know the cost you have borne,
the body broken, the blood outpoured,
love stretched to the limit, yet victorious.

15   Mountain prayer

Luke 9:18–36

Jesus took with him Peter and John and James, and went up on the mountain to pray.
LUKE 9:28

Holy Spirit, fire of God
alongside us and within us,
take us further – further up and further in –
as we pray with Jesus, who prays for us.
Take us further,
as we gaze on his face, bright with love,
and are changed by his light shining upon us.
Take us further,
as we open the scriptures and hear
its word of liberation and its call upon our lives.
Take us further,
as we take up our cross day by day
and journey with Christ in the exodus,
which frees us from fear and oppression, from sin and death.

Holy Spirit, breath of God,
take us further,
as you rouse us from our heavy sleep
and open our eyes to the glory of Jesus.
Take us further,
as the mystery of God – the cloud of terror and joy –
overshadows, overwhelms and overpowers us.
Take us further,
as God speaks the word of life
and we are led to listen to the beloved.
Take us further,
as the vision fades and disappears,

and Jesus stands with us alone, now and always.
Take us further,
as we carry the wonder of grace and the challenge of truth
into the ordinary world of work and money, home and family,
time and travel, politics and lifestyle, laughter and tears.

16   The peace mission

Luke 10:1–16

'Whatever house you enter, first say, "Peace to this house!"'
LUKE 10:5

Send us out, Lord,
into our streets and neighbourhoods,
into our villages and towns,
our cities and nations,
our world, with all its deep beauty and brutal pain.
Send us out, Lord,
into homes full of emptiness
and lives in need of your fullness.

Keep it simple, Lord.
Take from us
the burdens of status and pride,
position and possessions,
anxiety and fear.
Keep us true to you
and true to your way.

Fill us with your peace, Lord,
that grace and peace may flow:
flow through us to all we meet;
flow through talk at table
and words along the way;
flow through deeds of kindness
and messages of hope.
Fill us with your peace,
to bring healing to your world
and the nearness of your kingdom.

Stay with us, Lord,
that we may stay with others
in all that life brings:
the joy and the hardship,
the love and the hurt,
patiently, persistently sharing your life.

Shake from us, Lord,
the dust of cynicism and despair,
the dust of evil and hatred,
the dust of ignorance and folly.
Shake from us
the dust of self-sufficiency and human pride,
the dust that clogs hearts and minds and deadens life.

Turn us back, Lord,
to your joy,
your peace,
your word of life
that we may ever walk
in the light of your dawn.

17   Jesus rejoices

Luke 10:17–24

**At that same hour Jesus rejoiced in the Holy Spirit and said,
'I thank you, Father, Lord of heaven and earth…'**
LUKE 10:21

Rejoice, rejoice!
Our names are in heaven's light!
Our souls are kept in the Spirit's care!
Our lives are called to the work of Christ!

Rejoice, rejoice!
God's love cannot be grasped by human minds!
God's life cannot be trapped in human wisdom!
God's Spirit blows as it wills, gracious and free!

Rejoice, rejoice!
In Jesus Christ, who shows us the Father's heart!
In Jesus Christ, who declares us to be God's children!
In Jesus Christ, who calls us to follow his way!

Rejoice, rejoice!
In the Father's faithfulness,
in Jesus' joy,
in the Spirit's surprises,
grace upon grace!

Rejoice, rejoice!
Give thanks this day and each day,
for God's will is so gracious
and God's wisdom is so deep,
through Jesus Christ, the bringer of joy.

18   Christ in the dust

Luke 10:25–37

'A man was going down from Jerusalem…'
LUKE 10:30

Christ in the dust,
you lie there
stripped of all dignity
with dark blood seeping from jagged wounds:
are you dead?

Christ in the dust,
have I passed by
like the priest and the Levite,
busy with my life,
afraid to get involved?

Christ in the dust,
thank you for the brave ones
who reach out in utter compassion,
forgetting the risk or the cost,
tending your wounds, anointing your body,
lifting you up and bringing you to a safe place.

Christ in the dust,
confront me with my fears and indifference,
and by your Spirit, stir up within me
true love, deep compassion and determined action,
that I may love my neighbour as myself,
love them as you love me.

19   Martha and Mary

Luke 10:38–42

… a woman named Martha welcomed him into her home. She had a sister named Mary, who sat at the Lord's feet…
LUKE 10:38–39

Lord Jesus,
we thank you for Martha, the hospitable one,
　　and we thank you for Mary, who listened and learnt your way.
We honour them and all women of love and faith,
　　and we seek to be open to your coming,
　　your word to us and your way for our lives.
Lord Jesus,
　　we invite you into our homes,
　　the places of our being.
We have much to do:
　　show us what we must do and what we must set aside.
We have many things:
　　show us how to share what we have and to let go of that
　　　　which possesses us.
We are surrounded by events and voices and noise:
　　help us to listen for your voice, your word, your silence.
Lord Jesus,
we are anxious about our lives, worried and distracted over
　　many things:
　　help us to centre our hearts on the way of your kingdom,
　　to carry your peace in our being
　　and to make peace in our world.

20 Lord teach us to pray

Luke 11:1–4

He was praying in a certain place...
LUKE 11:1

Lord, teach us to pray
with the whole of our being,
    bodies stilled and centred,
    minds focused on your way,
    hearts warmed by your grace.

Lord, teach us to pray
with the whole of your people,
    connecting to your followers of every time and place,
    connecting to your church in all its varied faces,
    connecting to the world with all its joy and agony.

Lord, teach us to pray
in the power of your Spirit,
    as children of one dear God,
    as brothers and sisters in Christ,
    as sinners forgiven and forgiving.

Lord, teach us to pray
    to you,
    with you,
    in you,
    this moment,
    this life,
    this eternity.

21   Friend indeed

Luke 11:5–13

'… knock and the door will be opened for you.'
LUKE 11:9

My friend,
I knock and knock,
embarrassed by the echoing sound at this late hour,
anxious of what the neighbours may think,
worried that you may not come,
that the door will remain closed to my hammering.
I stand and wait,
listening for signs of your wakefulness,
sounds from within your dwelling,
the rattle of bolts, the echoes of footsteps.
I call out, I plead,
unsure of my own voice,
yet desperate that you may hear my cry.
I shout,
though the scream is silent within me.
I am hungry,
hungry for the bread you alone can give,
thirsty for that word you alone can speak.
Open the door… open the door… open the door.
Give me bread, not just enough for myself,
but bread that I can share with the hungry people,
your thirsty children.
Do not sleep, my friend.
Do not ignore my call.
Open the door… open the door… open the door.

My friend, you come.
I hear your step, your voice from within.
You come, and I am overwhelmed by the life you give,
the joy you share, the hunger you satisfy.
The door has been opened.
The bread has been broken.
Thank you, God of grace, my friend indeed.

22   Let us look

Luke 12:22–34

'Consider the ravens… Consider the lilies…'
LUKE 12:24, 27

Let us be still and turn from our anxious thoughts and petty
schemes and let us look.
Let us, by the Spirit's power, look again and look deep.
Let us look at nature with all its strange wonders.
Look at the birds in speedy flight or searching patiently for
seeds or worms, nesting in the tall trees
or simply singing for delight.
Look at the meadow grass with its spectrum of greens,
dotted with colours enough for Joseph's coat.
Look at the wildflowers – their rich colours, curving shapes
and delicate textures, far surpassing Solomon's finery
or any designer clothes of today.
Look at nature and see God's hand in creating and sustaining
moment by moment, the very fabric of existence.

Let us look at ourselves and the foolishness of our lives – our
attempts to control all, to have all, to know all.
Look and laugh at our folly.
Look and change our ways.

Let us look at God, who like a loving parent holds and feeds,
knows all our needs, from the basics of bread and warmth
to the more basics of love and purpose.
Look at God, the invisible one made visible in Jesus.
Look and give thanks for the Creator's care,
the Saviour's love, the Spirit's help.

Let us look for signs of God's kingdom – to seek that joyful reality
above all else.
Look and pray and work and strive for that just peace
that is God's way,
for our world
and for our lives.

23   Lost sheep

Luke 15:1–7

'Rejoice with me, for I have found my sheep that was lost.'
LUKE 15:6

God whose likeness we bear,
you never cease to search us out,
never cease to look for your lost children,
the sheep of your flock.
And when at last we are found in you,
you carry us on your shoulders,
singing and triumphant.
You draw others into the celebration
and spread your joy through heaven itself.
So, dear Lord, seek out your lost sheep of today.
Despite the pain and the cost,
enter the hard places of this earth, the places
   where hope has died,
   where faith is mocked,
   where love is abused.
Call those found in you to follow you there
to share the work of search and rescue
in the name of Jesus,
the shepherd who gave himself to the wolves
that we might live.

24 A woman and a coin

Luke 15:8–10

'What woman having ten silver coins, if she loses one of them, does not light a lamp, sweep the house, and search carefully until she finds it?'
LUKE 15:8

Holy Spirit, sweep through the dust of my life:
    Come down, O Love Divine,
    seek thou this soul of mine.
Lighten the darkness that surrounds me
and the darkness within me;
expose my false ways and foolish pride:
    Come down, O Love Divine,
    seek thou this soul of mine.
Sweep through the dust and debris,
the accumulation of knowledge and memory and possession;
expose my childlike vulnerability:
    Come down, O Love Divine,
    seek thou this soul of mine.
Find me, lift me up, restore me
to wholeness and hope
to the purpose you have for me:
    Come down, O Love Divine,
    seek thou this soul of mine.
The search is over!
Celebrate your find, your victory!
I am yours and you are mine:
    Come down, O Love Divine,
    seek thou this soul of mine.
Dwell within me, Holy Spirit, my love and my joy.

25   Coming to our senses

Luke 15:11-24

'Let us eat and celebrate; for this son of mine was dead and is alive again; he was lost and is found!'
LUKE 15:23-24

We have taken our Father's inheritance.
Outgrown the divine care, we go our own way.
Escaping God's home,
we attempt to make our own world.
With abandon we spend creation's riches,
bringing desert where once the forests stood so proud
and melting icecaps with our heat.
People are hungry – hungry for food, for love, for hope;
and we watch, distant and helpless,
knowing our own emptiness.

Where shall we go?
Faith looks like slavery, a set of rules and rituals,
bitter guilt and hard duty.
Surely we are free and glad to be?
Yet our minds ache and our minds are unsettled.
We seek all the securities, insurance for the future
and reassurance for the now.
We fill our lives with more and more,
but still stay empty.

But is there another way?
What if we come to our senses?
What if we journey back to God, who is already coming to meet us?
What if we allow ourselves to be embraced by God?
What if we share in God's feast of hope and celebration?

The lost can be found.
The dead can rise to new life.
Thanks be to God.

26   The older son

Luke 15:25–32

'Then the father said to him, "Son, you are always with me,
and all that is mine is yours. But we had to celebrate and
rejoice, because this brother of yours was dead and has come
to life; he was lost and has been found."'

LUKE 15:31–32

Father, who is a stranger to me,
I stand outside and refuse to come in,
angry at your foolish love for my brother,
jealous of the joy that son of yours has received from you,
doubtful that you love me in that way,
resentful of the dutiful faith I have pursued all these years,
suspicious that the celebration will cost me dear.
I stand outside and refuse to come in.

So Father, so full of strange grace,
you come out to meet me,
reaching out with that same foolish love,
calling me child, giving me all
and calling me to share in the celebration
of the lost who are found,
the dead who are raised to new life.

Father, always with me,
I who have travelled nowhere in my faith am lost.
I who have risked nothing in my love am dead.
I stand outside, but want to come in.
Restore me to yourself, renew your life within me.
Take from me my anger, jealousy, doubt, resentment
    and suspicion,
and bring me home, that I may know your joy
and share in the banquet of your grace and mercy.

27   Children of Abraham

Luke 16:19–31

'At his gate lay a poor man named Lazarus, covered with sores.'
LUKE 16:20

Father Abraham,
remind us of our place within your family,
your covenant of blessing for all the families of the earth.
Keep the gates of our hearts open to our sisters and brothers
    in poverty.

Brother Moses,
point us to the great 'I am', who hears the cry of the people,
knows their suffering and comes to their rescue.
Open our ears to the cries of those enslaved today.

Great prophets of the past and the present,
confront us with your righteous anger at the bitter injustices
    of our time.
Open our minds to your message of restoration and renewal.

Brother Lazarus, dying in poverty yet raised to glory,
humble us in our self-seeking lives, our complacent well-being.
Bring us repentance and open our lives to new hope.

Lord Jesus, the one who rose from the dead
and can bring new life to all,
free us from all that binds us
and lead us in your way of sacrificial love and fierce compassion.

28   Were not ten healed?

Luke 17:11–19

Then one of them, when he saw that he was healed, turned back, praising God with a loud voice.
LUKE 17:15

Lord Jesus,
you have seen us as we are,
in need of your grace and mercy.
You have healed us,
restoring us to life itself.
You have saved us
from ourselves and our fears
and the grip of evil.
You have rescued us
and led us to new joy and hope.

What can we give in return?
Yes, our obedience to your word to us,
yet we know that obedience is not enough.
In the face of your grace,
praise and thanksgiving alone are sufficient,
poured out at your feet, in wonder and love.

So we raise our voices
in worship and joy,
seeing all that you have done and all that you are.
Accept our love and praise this day
and then send us on our way,
made whole by your mercy.

29   Widow's plea

Luke 18:1–8

'And will not God grant justice to his chosen ones who cry to him day and night?'
LUKE 18:7

God of justice,
renew our faith in you
and our commitment to your kingdom:
your just rule,
where widows are heard and comforted,
the oppressed set free, the poor given hope.
Confront the injustice of our times
and give us courage to voice your outrage.

God of tenderness,
console and guard us,
that we may not lose heart
when your kingdom seems so distant,
your will so resisted.
Touch us with the tears of the outcasts,
the victims of the world's greed and carelessness.
Keep us praying,
and keep us working for you.

God of urgent love,
hear our cry for this planet and its people.
Do not delay in helping us.
Do not let hope die.
Do not keep your Spirit from us.
Come to our aid and the aid of all your creation.

We pray in the name of the victim of injustice, who will bring true
    justice, our crucified and risen Lord, Jesus Christ.

30   The Pharisee's prayer

Luke 18:9–30

**'Two men went up to the temple to pray, one a Pharisee and
the other a tax-collector.'**
LUKE 18:10

I met Jesus today.
Yes I, the Pharisee, met Jesus today,
and he brought me to my knees.
I had stood before God and had felt so proud,
so content in my strong faith;
my goodness – in this rotten world;
my light – compared to others' darkness.
I had stood and remembered all I had achieved,
all the work I had done,
all the offerings I had given,
all the little sacrifices I had made for my god.

I met Jesus today,
and he showed me that my god
had nothing to do with the living God;
my light was darkness
when exposed to his fire;
my goodness empty and rotten to the core
in the fierce light of his goodness.

I met Jesus today,
and he made me look again –
   look again at God in all that awesome love and that fearsome
      truth;
   look again at that person I had looked down upon,
   treated with contempt or simply passed by;
   look at myself and my need of love.

I met Jesus today,
and he asked me to become like a little child,
a baby in the arms of God,
and it brought me to my knees –
God be merciful to me a sinner.

31   The one who seeks

Luke 19:1–10

'Today salvation has come to this house, because he too is a son of Abraham.'
LUKE 19:9

I am small,
amid the teeming millions of this world,
spinning in a space that grows ever larger.
I am small,
yet I seek you, THE GREAT ONE.
I climb to look beyond my crowded life,
scanning the horizon for the stirred dust of your approach.
And here I meet you.
You speak your word,
inviting me to my own home,
inviting me to know you, where I am.

I come eagerly to greet you, THE GRACIOUS ONE,
who has come into my midst and into my heart.
I am rich, yet lost.
There is so much to repair and repay,
so much injustice of which I am part.
Yet you kindly, gloriously accept
my fumbling attempts to make good.
You claim me as a child of Abraham,
part of your family, a brother-sister dear to you.

Thank you, THE SEEKING ONE,
who became poor that I might be truly rich,
and lost your life that I might find mine, in you.

32   Lament over Jerusalem

Luke 19:28–48

'If you, even you, had only recognised on this day the things that make for peace!'
LUKE 19:42

If only, if only, if only...

Is it too late for us, Lord,
    to make peace in the Middle East, Jew and Arab, Christian
       and Muslim,
    to make peace in Africa, black and white, rich and poor,
    to make peace with justice for all,
    to make peace with our planet?

Is it too late for us, Lord,
    to abandon our fears and our hatreds,
    to abandon the arms trade with all its profit,
    to abandon the corruptions, the lies, the posturing, the pride
       and the greed,
    to abandon the careless exploitation of our planet?

Is it too late for us, Lord,
    to welcome you, the one who rode into Jerusalem in humble
       peace,
    to weep with you, the one who wept for your city,
    to watch with you, the one who gave life on a cross,
    to walk with you, the one who goes before us?

Is it too late for us, Lord,
    to speak out for the voiceless,
    to speak out against the forces of fear,
    to speak out for a better, humbler way?

Is it too late for us, Lord?

Lord touch our hearts with your tears,
    strengthen our hands for your work,
    and guide our feet into the path of peace,
    that it may not be too late for us
    and this world you so love.

33 Rejected cornerstone

Luke 20:1—21:38

'Then the owner of the vineyard said, "What shall I do? I will send my beloved son; perhaps they will respect him."'
LUKE 20:13

The powers that be
are at work,
plotting and suppressing,
devising and insinuating.
But you, great teacher,
will not be taken in,
not impressed by self-made glory,
the boasts of holiness,
the size of our towers and temples.
You come as the rescuer,
to turn the tables on greed and injustice,
on fear and death itself.
Lighten our darkness.
Come, Lord Jesus.

34   The desire of Christ

Luke 22:1–38

**He said to them, 'I have eagerly desired to eat this Passover
with you before I suffer.'**
LUKE 22:15

This is your deep desire, dear Lord:
to celebrate the Passover with us,
where you yourself are the sacrificial lamb;
to feed us with bread broken
and wine poured out and poured out again;
to feed us with your very self
for us to do with what we will,
to absorb into our very being,
to carry into our daily living,
if that is what we desire.

Forgive us our slowness to receive,
    our false promises and failed courage,
    our little denials and petty quarrels,
    our concern for our own status,
    our unwillingness to give and serve
in the face of your overwhelming love.
Forgive us and restore us to yourself.
Pray for us that our faith may not fail,
that we may turn back to you
and strengthen our brothers and sisters.

Grant that we may eat at your table
in the company of all your frail disciples
of every time and place,
now in our own day
and in the day your kingdom is fulfilled.

35   Sleeping?

Luke 22:39–46

'Why are you sleeping? Get up and pray…'
LUKE 22:46

Are we sleepwalking through reality, dear Lord?
Closing our eyes to your suffering in the betrayed ones,
the starving ones, the forgotten ones?
Turning our backs on your call to face evil head-on,
to confront injustice, to act to rescue this darkened world?

Are we sleepwalking through reality, dear Lord?
Preferring trivial games to the real task of living?
Opting for the comfortable way, the easy half-truths,
reassuring platitudes and false hopes?
Forgetting the cost of grace?

Are we sleepwalking through reality, dear Lord?
Taking all we can get from this planet
and betraying generations to come?
Prolonging our lives to the nth degree
and failing to give life to others?

Are we sleepwalking through reality, dear Lord?
Afraid to own that grief and fear we feel?
Afraid to hope for greater things,
that dying love that lives?

Wake us up, Lord of Gethsemane.
Challenge our feeble praying with your mighty prayer,
'Not my will but yours be done.'
Shame our selfishness.
We pray that we may not face the testing you endured.

But we pray too for strength and purpose
to meet whatever life may bring,
to meet it with faith and courage
and that grace you knew and shared
in a garden long ago.

36   The hour

Luke 22:47—23:56

'But this is your hour, and the power of darkness!'
LUKE 22:53

Lord Jesus,
the hour is not yours.
It is the hour of the powerful,
the violent, the corrupt;
an hour when you are seized
and taken, led away, denied,
mocked and beaten,
blindfolded and insulted.
You are sent back and forth,
the sport of mockers.
Your fate lies in the whim of the crowd
and the calculation of a weak politician.
You are condemned,
led away to be put to death,
stripped of your clothing,
nailed to a cross.
This hour is not yours.
It is the hour of darkness,
Where even the sun's light fails.
Yet…
Yet through the failure of Peter,
we see your look of compassion.
Over the mocking voices,
we hear your words of forgiveness.
In your searing pain,
we glimpse your promise of paradise.
In the darkest hour,
we know your innocence.

In your silence,
we hear God's whisper of love.
In your utter powerlessness
we see the power of God.
This is your hour of triumph!
This is your hour of victory!
Thanks be to God!

37   Remember

Luke 24:1–12

Then they remembered his words.
LUKE 24:8

God of faithful love,
we remember with thanks Mary Magdalane, Joanna, Mary the
    mother of James and the other women with them, as the
    great witnesses of Christ's death and resurrection.

We remember with thanks the women as they watched their
    Saviour die,
standing at a distance in the horror of it all.
We remember with thanks the women as they saw the newly cut
    tomb
and the way the limp body of Jesus was laid out within it.
We remember with thanks the women as they gathered spices
    and ointments,
grinding and mixing in preparation for their loving duty.
We remember with thanks the women as they rested on
    the sabbath,
obedient to the law, exhausted with grief and despair.
We remember with thanks the women as they rose early that
    first day,
coming with heavy hearts to the tomb of the beloved.
We remember with thanks the women as they discovered the
    tomb empty
and stepped within its cold walls, seeing that the body was gone.
We remember with thanks the women as they bowed their faces
before the awesome messengers of life, dazzling and terrifying.
We remember with thanks the women as they heard the
    message
'Christ has risen' and recalled his promises.

We remember with thanks the women as they told their story
and astounded their friends.
We remember with thanks the women as they held to their
    testimony,
despite the mockery and unbelief of the eleven and the rest.

God of new life,
guard us from
    forgetting your Easter good news,
    closing our minds to your resurrection truth,
    hardening our hearts to our risen Lord.
By your refreshing Spirit,
help us to share the women's wondrous joy and deep hope,
that we too may tell the news of the living one.

38   Emmaus Road

Luke 24:13–35

**While they were talking and discussing, Jesus himself came
near and went with them.**
LUKE 24:15

Why, Jesus?
Why are our hopes shattered?
Why such sadness, such suffering?
Why do you walk with us as a stranger?
Why are our eyes closed to your presence?

Yes, Jesus,
our hearts are foolish and slow to believe;
our ears are deaf to the witness of your people;
our Bibles remain closed, despite all we read;
we fail to meet you through its pages.

Yes, Jesus,
open the scriptures to us.
Make our hearts burn within us,
as the words become alive and real
and as you draw us to yourself.

Stay, Jesus,
it is almost evening and the day is nearly done.
Share at our table, take the bread and bless it.
Break it and meet our need
and make yourself known in the breaking.

Go, Jesus,
go before us on our journey
and help us to tell others
of the fire that burns within us
and how you fed us with the living bread.

39   History's hinge

Luke 24:44–52 (and Acts 1:1–14)

They worshipped him, and returned to Jerusalem with great joy; and they were continually in the temple blessing God.
LUKE 24:52

We return to the familiar place,
the holy temple,
with all its history,
all its hopes and disasters,
all its glory – true and false;
the stones impregnated with prayer
yet tainted with injustice and exclusion.
'Will God indeed dwell on the earth?'
    We come to praise our Lord, the righteous one,
    to thank our God, who has acted,
    without question, beyond all human grasp.

We return to the familiar place,
remembering all our Lord did and said within its precincts day
    after day,
his anger at the traders, the robbers of the poor,
his powerful words and fearsome challenges,
his courage in the face of death threats and plots.
'The stone that the builders rejected has become the cornerstone.'
    We come to praise our Lord, the living stone,
    to thank our God, who acts,
    bringing life from death, victory from defeat.

We return to the familiar place,
yet we are different.
We know God is true and real,
not bound to past history, but living and life-giving,
filling us with joy and hope.
The way is open before us.
'The curtain of the temple was torn in two.'
    We come to praise our Lord, the righteous one,
    to thank our God, who will act,
    sending that Spirit which we seek
    and for which we wait in worship.

40   Breakthrough

Luke 24:49; Acts 2:1–18

All of them were filled with the Holy Spirit…
ACTS 2:4

Come, Holy Spirit,
break into our lives,
gently or fiercely,
with reassurance or challenge, grace or truth.

Come, Holy Spirit,
burn in our hearts,
awakening love, releasing faith, warming love.

Come, Holy Spirit,
blow through our senses,
unsettling our cosy, comfortable ways,
sending us out to share wonder and to give praise.

Come, Holy Spirit,
reawaken your people,
demolishing the walls of division
and uniting all in vision and action.

Come, Holy Spirit,
speak in our world
a language that unites, instead of dividing,
a word of peace, instead of war,
a sound of joy, instead of fear.

Come, Holy Spirit,
in power and love,
joy and wonder,
challenge and grace.
Come and stay,
the embrace of God
on our lives today. Amen.

4

Praying with John

For John the focus has shifted from Jesus' announcement and teaching about God's kingdom to the person of Jesus himself. Much of the teaching recorded in the three synoptic gospels is absent; instead John focuses on signs by which Jesus 'revealed his glory', linking these to reflections on the person and saving work of Jesus, shown above all in the great 'I am' sayings. The gospel remains rooted in the historical events surrounding Jesus' life, death and resurrection, but has the nature of a profound meditation on these events and on Jesus himself. The writer concludes by telling his readers:

> Now Jesus did many other signs in the presence of his disciples, which are not written in this book. But these are written so that you may come to believe that Jesus is the Messiah, the Son of God, and that through believing you may have life in his name.
> JOHN 20:30–31

The purpose of the gospel is to strengthen the reader's trust and confidence in Jesus, as 'the way, and the truth, and the life' (John 14:6). Prayer plays its part in expressing this trust. Jesus prays to his

God and Father, in part as an expression of his deep and intimate relationship with the Father and in part to help and encourage his followers. His prayer first and foremost is, 'Father, glorify your name' (John 12:28). That glory is seen in the miracles and signs that Jesus performs but above all in the mystery of the cross, the self-giving love of Christ for the world. It is a glory that the Father shares with the Son and the Son gives to the Father, a mutual relationship into which Jesus' followers are enabled to enter by the Spirit – the Spirit of Jesus. This loving relationship opens up a joy that makes their joy complete and a peace that the world cannot give.

This glory has compassion and care for others at its heart. In a story unique to John, Jesus on the night of his arrest takes off his outer garments and washes his disciples' feet, giving them an example to follow of humble and gracious service.

Later that evening, Jesus prays for his present and future disciples, that they may be one, 'that the world may believe' (John 17:21). He prays that the love between Father and Son may take root within his followers, enabling them to reflect his life in their lives. Prayer in John's gospel is primarily about deepening that loving relationship in Christ. Jesus speaks of his being the true vine and his disciples as the branches; their task is simply to remain united to him, the main stem: 'abide in me as I abide in you' (John 15:4). To dwell in Christ is to share in his work of love in the world. Prayer then becomes a matter of solidarity and identity with Christ, rather than seeking our own way. It takes its focus in the new commandment that Jesus gives his disciples then and now: 'love one another as I have loved you' (John 15:12).

1   The beginning

John 1:1–18

In the beginning was the Word, and the Word was with God, and the Word was God.

JOHN 1:1

So this is how it all begins,
God who is mystery and life.
Here in your creative Word,
forming being from nothing, life in all its wonder
    and exuberance;
here in your living Word,
bringing light into every human heart;
here you come among us,
as Word made flesh and blood,
the cry of a child born in the night,
the touch of a hand,
the sparkle of eyes,
the smile of grace,
bread broken, wine poured out,
blood shed,
new life given.

We praise you, the God who comes to us in the life of Jesus.
We praise you, the God whose Spirit breathes into us true life.
We praise you, the God who formed the universe from nothing,
releasing life and new life and life for evermore.

2   John the Baptist

John 1:19–34

**He said, 'I am the voice of one crying out in the wilderness,
"Make straight the way of the Lord."'**

JOHN 1:23

God of all light,
we thank you for John,
who was not the light,
but pointed to the brilliant radiance of Jesus Christ.
We thank you for John,
who was not the Word,
but cried out in the wilderness,
clearing the path to life in you.
We thank you for John,
who was not the Messiah, the Christ,
but witnessed to your Spirit settling on Jesus,
like a dove making its nest.
We thank you for John,
who baptised with just water,
but directed us to the one who immerses us with your Spirit.
We thank you for John,
who was not the lamb to carry our burdens,
yet pointed to the one who takes the sin of the world
and throws it into the sea of your forgiving love.
We thank you for John,
who was not this or that,
but played his part, faithful and true.
We honour him for all he did,
and the cost he bore.
We thank you and seek to hear his witness
and to follow his way to Jesus, his Lord and ours.

3   Come and see

John 1:39, 43–51

Nathanael said to him, 'Can anything good come out of Nazareth?' Philip said to him, 'Come and see.'

JOHN 1:46

Come and see, you say,
yet our feet are slow to follow
this path and meet you, Lord.
Come and see, you say,
but our eyes are blurred,
our vision darkened.
Come and see, you say,
but we go our own way
and walk a lonely path.
Come and see, you say,
but assumptions crowd in:
'Can anything good come from Nazareth?'
Come and see, you say.

We come to you, Lord Jesus,
for you know our name
and see our need
and meet us where we are.
We glimpse your presence,
your life among us, within us, before us.
We reach out and touch your truth.
You are the true image of God,
the just peacemaker for the nations,
the mighty Saviour of the world.

4   Signpost

John 2:1-12

**Jesus did this, the first of his signs, in Cana of Galilee,
and revealed his glory; and his disciples believed in him.**
JOHN 2:11

In the midst of human celebration
you reveal your glory, Lord Jesus Christ.
The sign of plain water transformed into the best of wine
speaks of the new life you bring.
The part played by the servants in the task,
speaks of your drawing us into your work.
The surprise of the steward as he drinks the glorious wine
speaks of your most wondrous gift.
You came to bring life and life in abundance.
You came to show love and love divine.
You came to share joy and joy that was complete.
You came to give peace, a peace no one else could give.
You came to face your hour and pour out your life for all.
We praise you for your first sign, a miracle of grace,
a pointer to your work in our world that longs for hope.
We will taste your wine and drink it deep.
We will know your power within us,
like branches drawing strength from the vine.
The water there to clean our bodies
has been turned to wine to refresh our souls,
a taste of heaven among us.
Thank you, Lord Jesus.

5   The new temple

John 2:13–25

**Jesus answered them, 'Destroy this temple, and in three days
I will raise it up.'**
JOHN 2:19

Will you dwell with us,
God who is spirit and truth?
Will you meet us in our world
of concrete, glass and steel,
of many faiths and sacred spaces,
of grief and exploitation,
hopes and longings?
Will you let us enter your presence,
with all your vast mystery and wondrous glory?
Will you clear a path through all our turning
and twisting of your way?

Come, Spirit, lead us to the new temple.
Come, lead us into the life of Jesus.
Come, lead us into the burning heart of our God.

6   Rebirth

John 3:1–15

He came to Jesus by night and said to him, 'Rabbi, we know that you are a teacher who has come from God...'
JOHN 3:2

God of rebirth,
we thank you for Nicodemus,
bound by background and situation,
but seeking all the same to know more of you and of Jesus.
We thank you for his questions,
his honest confusion,
his willingness to listen and to learn.
We thank you for that night long ago
when he touched your presence,
glimpsed your kingdom
and began a journey
towards rebirth by your Spirit.
We thank you for his presence in the story of Jesus,
not only on that wondrous, puzzling night,
but later in the deeper darkness of Jesus' arrest, death
    and burial.
We thank you for the spices he brought to the tomb of Jesus,
sufficient for the burial of a king,
another footstep in his journey to your kingdom.
Work in our lives, great God,
that we too may enter your kingdom,
reborn as your much-loved children,
brothers and sisters of Jesus.

7   God's increase

John 3:22–36

'He must increase, but I must decrease.'
JOHN 3:30

God who is more true than we can ever grasp,
we thank you that the waters of heaven flow deep and pure,
sparkling with your truth, teeming with your vibrant life,
open to all who receive the gracious gift of your Spirit,
the life of your Son in our midst.

God who is life beyond all life,
make space within us for your work today.
Push back our stubborn egos, our guilt and pride,
that the life of Christ may grow and flourish.
Open our minds to the voice of Jesus
and pour out your Spirit that cannot be contained.
So may your joy and truth, your love and life,
increase within us, this and every day.

8 Living water

John 4:1–42

A Samaritan woman came to draw water, and Jesus said to her, 'Give me a drink'.

JOHN 4:7

God of abundant life,
we thank you for the unnamed Samaritan woman
who gave Jesus water and asked him for living water.
We bring to heart and mind the woman who today has walked
   many miles to fetch water for herself and her family, facing
   danger, discomfort and disease:
   may your living water flow through her life.
We bring to heart and mind the woman who today has been
   excluded or abused simply because of her race or religion:
   may your living water flow through her life.
We bring to heart and mind the woman who today struggles with
   relationships that have gone wrong and all their after-effects:
   may your living water flow through her life.
We bring to heart and mind the woman who today seeks to
   worship you in whatever place that might be:
   may your living water flow through her life.
We bring to heart and mind the woman who today has witnessed
   to Jesus as the one who spoke to her heart, and so brings his
   life to those around her:
   may your living water flow through her life.
God of abundant life,
we thank you for these unnamed women of today.
   May your living water flow through them and us.

9   The second sign

John 4:43–54

**Jesus said to him, 'Go; your son will live.' The man believed the
word that Jesus spoke to him and started on his way.**
JOHN 4:50

Father of all,
the second sign goes unnoticed, eclipsed by the water turned
    into wine.
Yet here again, you point us to life made new.
Here is sickness turned into wholeness,
despair turned into hope,
desperation turned to trust,
death turned into life.
These are signs of your kingdom,
signs of Jesus at work,
signs that your Son lives.
We pray in the name of your Son,
who died on the cross and who lives.
Turn our doubt into faith.
Use our hopes and longings for new life,
our prayers for the world,
that the fever of hatred and violence may be finally banished
and wholeness come, in all its grace and splendour.

10   Jesus the questioner

John 5:1–18

One man was there who had been ill for thirty-eight years. When Jesus saw him lying there and knew that he had been there a long time, he said to him, 'Do you want to be made well?'

JOHN 5:5–6

Lord Jesus,
you are the questioner,
prodding our hearts and minds with your words.
You are the one who sees our sickness and our need.
You are the one who asks us if we truly want to be made whole,
to be healed of all that traps us.
Forgive us our excuses, our blaming of others for what we are.
Forgive us our failure to see ourselves
with the love with which you look on us.
Forgive us our slowness to accept all you give.
Ask your probing questions.
Take from us all that misguides and distorts.
Speak your word of hope and challenge.
Raise us to our feet to walk your way.

11   Nothing lost

John 6:1–40

So they gathered them up, and from the fragments of the five barley loaves, left by those who had eaten, they filled twelve baskets.

JOHN 6:13

God who feeds the hungry,
we thank you for the barley loaves and fishes offered long ago
and the hands of Jesus taking and blessing them for your work.
So may every small gift offered today be multiplied by
   your grace.
May every crumb be gathered to feed your people.
May nothing be wasted of all you give
in the economics of heaven.
May signs of your kingdom be glimpsed
in every corner of our globe.
May Christ lose nothing in the work you have entrusted to him,
to give new life to the world,
life that loves and lasts, now and forever.

12   Words of eternal life

John 6:41–71

Simon Peter answered him, 'Lord, to whom can we go? You have the words of eternal life.'
JOHN 6:68

Flesh-and-blood Jesus,
forgive us when we seek
a more comfortable Christ,
a man-made Messiah
who confirms our way of thinking
and questions nothing in our lives.

Sent-from-the-Father Jesus,
forgive us when we turn away
from your cross in all its harsh reality,
unwilling to face its pain and violence.

Bread-of-life Jesus,
forgive us when we pick at your teaching,
refusing to name our hunger
and feed on your outpoured love.

Spirit-filled Jesus,
do not turn us away,
for you have the words of eternal life,
and we know there is no other way.

13   Divisions deepen

John 7:1–52

Now he said this about the Spirit, which believers in him were to receive; for as yet there was no Spirit, because Jesus was not yet glorified.

JOHN 7:39

Release your Spirit, God of glory,
    that divisions of the past may be healed
    and the conflicts of today move on towards peace.
Release your Spirit, God of glory,
    that the teaching of Jesus
    may reach new minds and hearts.
Release your Spirit, God of glory,
    that fresh signs of the Messiah at work
    may be seen in our land and our times.
Release your Spirit, God of glory,
    that the Jesus of Palestine
    may be known as the Christ of every place and time.
Release your Spirit, God of glory,
    that the deep thirst within all humanity
    may be quenched by your living water.
Release your Spirit, God of glory,
    that every deception, every half-truth
    and hateful lie may be exposed
    and the shocking, shattering truth of Jesus proclaimed anew.

14   Words in the sand

John 7:53—8:11

Jesus bent down and wrote with his finger on the ground.
JOHN 8:6

What did you write in the sand, Lord Jesus,
that day when angry men
dragged that terrified woman before you?
Your teaching interrupted
and expectation in the air,
would you condemn or look away?
What could you say?
The law of Moses had given its command,
and stones lay ready at hand.
But you spoke a new word,
turning the eyes of angry men
away from the woman to their own hearts and souls:
'Let the one without sin
be the first to throw a stone.'
The noise and hubbub quietened,
the crowd grew silent,
and one by one the men, who had been so ready
to carry out the sentence, slipped away.
And all the while you wrote in the sand.
A word of grief over hard hearts?
A word of hope for new beginnings?
A word of mercy and love?
A word to change the world?
What will you write on our hearts this day, Lord Jesus?

15   Radiance

John 8:12–30

**Again Jesus spoke to them, saying, 'I am the light of the world.
Whoever follows me will never walk in darkness but will have
the light of life.'**
JOHN 8:12

Lights blaze across our planet,
polluting night's gentle darkness,
confusing birds and nature's nocturnal creatures.
Lights blaze across our planet,
speaking of human power and invention,
the reckless dominance of this young and foolish species.
Lights blaze around us,
turning our night into day.
Yet, Lord, the darkness within remains,
a slavery centred on ourselves,
leading nowhere, crushing love, stifling life.
Bring your light into our darkness, living Lord.
Lead us to the truth that brings such freedom.
Lead us to the Father's presence that brings such joy.
Thank you for the light deeper than our blazing cities.
Thank you for the word that speaks of you.

16 Before Abraham

John 8:31–59

Jesus said to them, 'Very truly, I tell you, before Abraham was, I am.'
JOHN 8:58

God of Abraham and God of Jesus,
we turn to you as loving judge of all our words and actions.
We seek your wisdom as we hear your living word,
your help amid the controversy and anger of this passage.
Lead us, step by step, to that great affirmation,
that Jesus is beyond all human time,
the 'I am' even before Abraham, the father of the nations.
Lead us beyond the accusations of the past,
to know that truth that sets us free,
free from the slavery that distorts and deadens,
free to live with hope and joy.
So may we honour Abraham and Jesus
and be led by them into your presence and your glory.

17   Eyes opened

John 9:1–12

As he walked along, he saw a man blind from birth.
JOHN 9:1

God of all time,
we remember today an unnamed man,
blind from birth, still longing to see.
We remember the acceptance he found from Jesus,
not blamed or rejected but touched by love.
We remember the mud and the spit,
that messy, earthly reality that spoke of new creation.
We thank you for the word of Jesus,
sending the man to the pool
and his coming back to Jesus, to see his Saviour for the first time.
We thank you for this man's courage and honesty,
as he faced hostile questions
and his witness to that one thing,
that having been blind he now could see.
We thank you that he could see his Saviour
and say to Jesus, 'Lord, I believe.'

God of all time,
we who do not see
reach out in hope and longing
and with that unnamed man we say,
'Lord we believe' and trust in you.

18 The shepherd

John 10:1–21

'I am the good shepherd. The good shepherd lays down his life for the sheep.'
JOHN 10:11

Good shepherd,
you walk among us today,
longing for your flock to be one.
You laid down your life,
throwing yourself to the wolves,
that the sheep might be saved.
Hear our prayer for all who have been scattered,
desperate for safety in a new land.
Hear our prayer for all who have been wounded,
by injustice, violence, fear or cruelty.
Hear our prayer
for those seeking a better, truer life
and those who have lost their way.
Be their good shepherd;
bring life – abundant life – into our world once more.

19   One with the Father

John 10:22–42

'The Father and I are one.'
JOHN 10:30

In the stillness of this moment,
I enter your presence,
living God beyond all time and space.
I stand in the holy temple,
confronted by your glory and your grace.

In the stillness of this moment,
I hear a word, a whisper:
'The Father and I are one.'
The voice is deep and true.
It is the voice of Jesus.

Questions from the past hang in the air,
the debates of history and religion,
the tensions of belief and practice,
controversies that go deep,
formulas that go stale.
Yet still I hear that word, a whisper:
'The Father and I are one.'

In the stillness of this moment,
I hear the truth, I glimpse
the oneness of Father and Son,
the outpoured love that is the heart of God.
Praise be to you, Lord Jesus, one with the Father.
I stand on holy ground.

20   Tears

John 11:1–57

Jesus began to weep.
JOHN 10:35

Life of all life, with us in Jesus,
we hold before you
those approaching death,
those who sit with them
and those anxious for news.
Be with them all in their distress and waiting.
Listen to their confusion, anger and fears,
the blame they may place on you or others.
Accept them as they are,
but speak a new word in their hearts.
Weep with them,
as you wept out of love for Lazarus.
And when the time is right, declare your word of resurrection life,
your command to roll back the stone of death
and bring release and glory, the fragrance of hope in you.

21   Fragrance

John 12:1–11

The house was filled with the fragrance of the perfume.
JOHN 12:3

God of grace,
we remember a meal shared among friends,
in honour of Jesus the life-giver.
Martha serves and Lazarus is there.
Mary anoints the king who is to die
and sweet perfume fills the air.
Yet Judas, caught up in twisted words and bitter thoughts,
fails to breathe in its goodness.

God of grace,
drive away the stench of death, the stink of betrayal,
the reek of corruption and lies.
Fill our world with the fragrance of outpoured love,
the presence of your anointed one here among us.

22 God glorified

John 12:20–50

'Father, glorify your name.' Then a voice came from heaven, 'I have glorified it, and I will glorify it again.'
JOHN 12:28

Lord Jesus, we picture you on the cross,
a fragile seed sown in our world,
trampled and obliterated yet bearing a glorious harvest:
  for this we praise you.

Lord Jesus, we picture you on the cross,
a place where the world is judged… and saved,
evil is confronted… and victory is won:
  for this we praise you.

Lord Jesus, we picture you on the cross,
your hour for eternity, that moment of strange glory,
glory given to the Father:
  for this we praise you.

Lord Jesus, we picture you on the cross,
a sign of eternal love
that draws us to yourself:
  for this we praise you.

Lord Jesus, we want to see you in our world today
and to know your glory for evermore.

23   Foot washing

John 13:1–20

Then he poured water into a basin and began to wash the disciples' feet and to wipe them with the towel that was tied around him.
JOHN 13:5

Jesus, the teacher,
there, in a basin of water,
you show us your way:
the down-to-earth way of love,
made visible in hands bathing tired, dusty feet.

Still, like Peter, we fail to grasp
the wonder of what you do,
as your reach into the heart of life,
the dirt and smell of humanity.

Kneel before us now,
to humble and inspire,
to refresh and revive,
that we too may follow
your down-to earth way of love.

24   Betrayal and love

John 13:21–38

So, after receiving the piece of bread, he immediately went out. And it was night.

JOHN 13:30

All-seeing God,
was it a failure of love that night, when Judas left the room?
Had he hidden his face as Jesus spoke of betrayal?
Had the bread stuck in his throat as he received it from his Lord?
Did Satan really enter him at that moment as he tasted what
    was good?
Or was it some twisted thought that drove him on? Confusion
    or greed?
So many questions we would ask.

All-seeing God,
in the gospel story Judas is the villain, pure and simple.
Yet we thank you that on that dark night Jesus showed
    a different way.
He shares a new command to love as he has loved them.
He shares that love even knowing that Peter will deny him,
that Judas has gone out into the darkness
and that he will journey to the cross alone.

All-seeing God,
your love in Christ does not fail,
love, pure and simple,
there to change our lives for good.

25   The way

John 14:1–14

**Jesus said to him, 'I am the way, and the truth, and the life.
No one comes to the Father except through me.'**
JOHN 14:6

God of all creation, God of all humanity,
we thank you for calming our hearts
with the words of Jesus.
We hear the promise and assurance that he gives
that none come to you,
as children to a loving parent,
except through what he has done.
We will not let these words be used to threaten,
to exclude or to engender fear.
We know he came
to bring life, not death,
hope, not condemnation,
invitation, not exclusion.
So we come to you, through his self-giving love.
We see you, reflected in all he was and is,
all he said and did.
He is the way to your presence.
He is the truth that frees us from fear.
He is the life given not for a few,
but for the world,
life overflowing with your Spirit.
Thank you for Jesus, showing us the way.

26   The advocate

John 14:15–31

'But the Advocate, the Holy Spirit, whom the Father will send
in my name, will teach you everything, and remind you of all
that I have said to you.'

JOHN 14:26

With open hands,
we welcome you, Spirit of truth.
With open minds,
we hear new words, reminding us of Jesus.
With open hearts,
we receive the peace that only Christ can give.

Come, Spirit, help us now.
Come, Spirit, rise up within us.
Come, Spirit, let us be on our way,
the way of our Saviour and our Lord.

27   The true vine

John 15:1–27

**'I am the vine, you are the branches. Those who abide in me
and I in them bear much fruit, because apart from me you can
do nothing.'**
JOHN 15:5

Living God,
we are amazed and thankful that your vine is full of vibrant life,
carrying within it the life and breath of Christ,
bringing such fruit of healing and compassion,
love and peace to torn and broken lives.
We are amazed and thankful that Christ calls us to be part of that
    vine today,
resting and relying on his presence and his love.
We are amazed and thankful that he invites us to pray boldly in
    his name,
and share a joy that goes so deep.
We are amazed and thankful that he names us not as servants
    but as his friends,
choosing us to produce good fruit for the world.

So bind us close to the main stem that is Jesus.
Prune us of all that is at odds with his love.
Cut out the dead wood and let his life flow in and out of us,
bringing a joyful harvest of grace and peace,
the glorious fruit of your kingdom.

28   The advantage

John 16:1–33

**'Nevertheless, I tell you the truth: it is to your advantage that
I go away, for if I do not go away, the Advocate will not come
to you; but if I go, I will send him to you.'**
JOHN 16:7

Every advantage is ours, amazing God,
not because of education or wealth,
race or status, religion or technology, success or achievement.
The advantage comes from you.
The words of Jesus are there to remember always,
showing us where we come from
and to whom we belong;
showing us that death has been overcome,
tears and sorrow will come to an end.
The Spirit's gift is here, to lead us on,
to open new truths, new visions,
in a new time and changing world.

Come, Spirit, teach us the way of Jesus,
among neighbours of every faith and none.
Come, Spirit, teach us the wisdom of Jesus,
among global economics and the politics of fear.
Come, Spirit, teach us the love of Jesus,
in a world with all its advantages and all its desperate needs.

29   Jesus' prayer

John 17:1–26

After Jesus had spoken these words, he looked up to heaven and said, 'Father, the hour has come; glorify your Son so that the Son may glorify you.'
JOHN 17:1

Here is the deepest of prayers,
founded on a love older than time,
the love of the Father for the Son and the Son for the Father,
the love lived out in flesh and blood,
facing the hour of crisis,
the desolation and death on a cross,
yet the place of glory.

Here is the deepest of prayers,
as Jesus looks to heaven
and rests in the Father's love,
knowing the glory that is his to share.

Here is the deepest of prayers,
as Jesus prays protection for his followers
and unity amid all the conflicts and divisions of the world.
We join our prayers with his,
God who is one at heart,
Father, Son and Holy Spirit,
that today's followers may know
that love that binds all wounds
and makes us one.

30   The arrest

John 18:1–27

Again he asked them, 'For whom are you looking?' And they said, 'Jesus of Nazareth.'
JOHN 18:7

You stood alone, Lord Jesus,
in the garden that had been your place of safety and prayer.
You faced your betrayer in the darkness of that night,
the soldiers with their lanterns and their swords.
You sought the safety of your friends,
refusing to take the way of violence.
You let yourself be taken, held and bound,
led from Annas to Caiaphas to Pilate,
subject to their power games and their fears.

You stood alone, Lord Jesus,
and Simon Peter denied your place within his world.
Touch my heart with your lonely vigil,
your courage and your truth,
your oneness with all who suffer,
your oneness with their pain.

31   Truth and power

John 18:28–40

**Pilate asked him, 'So you are a king?' Jesus answered, 'You say
that I am a king. For this I was born, and for this I came into
the world, to testify to the truth. Everyone who belongs to the
truth listens to my voice.' Pilate asked him, 'What is truth?'**
JOHN 18:37

God of utter truth,
we wait and watch as Jesus, bound and beaten,
stands before Pilate on that darkened day.
What is it to be: power or truth?
Pilate knows about power,
the power of kings and emperors,
the power to release or execute,
life or death according to his whim.
He wants to know if Jesus is a king
and what his kingdom followers might do.
But the truth that Jesus speaks
leaves him puzzled and unsure.
'What is truth?' he says
and does not wait for an answer.
Yet wait we must,
listening for that voice that speaks the truth that sets all free:
truth confronting power in all its ugliness;
truth exposing hypocrisy and lies;
truth that leads us to the heart of God,
that reality of goodness that Pilate
glimpsed in the prisoner he met that day.

32   Crown of thorns

John 19:1–16

So Jesus came out, wearing the crown of thorns and the purple robe. Pilate said to them, 'Here is the man!'
JOHN 19:5

Here is our king, flogged and abused,
mocked with a crown of thorns and a borrowed robe.
   We praise you, Jesus, king of all.
Here is the man, presented to the crowd,
the one who shows us what a human being can be.
   We praise you, Jesus, true humanity.
Here is the Son of God, under sentence of death,
the life-giver, giving his life.
   We praise you, Jesus, one with God.
Here is the silent one,
who speaks God's power.
   We praise you, Jesus, the Word made flesh.
Here is the crucified king,
finishing the task.
   We praise you, Jesus; your work is complete.

33   Mother and son

John 19:17–27

When Jesus saw his mother and the disciple whom he loved standing beside her, he said to his mother, 'Woman, here is your son.' Then he said to the disciple, 'Here is your mother.'
JOHN 19:26–27

God of new beginnings,
we thank you for the cross of Christ,
rescuing the world from evil, defeating death,
showing the height and depth, breadth and length of your love,
humanity and divinity flowing like blood and water.

God of new beginnings,
we thank you for the words of Christ,
spoken, there and then, to a mother and a friend.
We thank you for this little detail,
amid the enormity of that moment,
the cosmic scale of Christ's work that day.
We thank you for the compassion Christ showed,
for a mother in deepest pain and a friend bereft.

God of new beginnings,
we thank you for the love of Christ,
that flowed out to Mary and to John,
empowering them to share new hope and life.

God of new beginnings,
make new sons and daughters, new mothers and fathers,
in your kingdom community,
this and every day.

34   Finished

John 19:28–42

**When Jesus had received the wine, he said, 'It is finished.'
Then he bowed his head and gave up his spirit.**
JOHN 19:30

Behold, death has done its worst,
and after the thirst and anguish
Jesus hangs limp, his spirit gone.
It is over, finished, done.
Onlookers watch and look away;
the crowd disperses.
The body is taken down;
a tomb and spices will mark the end.
'It is finished,' he said,
but not in defeat or despair.
No, this is a word of triumph.
It is complete; the task is done;
what was necessary has been accomplished;
the lamb that takes away the sin of the world
has done the deed.
And now life can start again:
the life of Christ among us
and our lives, made new in him.
Thank you, Jesus, for forgiveness won.
Thank you for finishing the labour of love.
Thank you for the costly victory of the cross.

35   The gardener

John 20:1–18

Jesus said to her, 'Woman, why are you weeping? For whom are you looking?'
JOHN 20:15

Amid the tears of this damaged, grieving world
you come, risen Lord, to open eyes and hearts to life made new.
Among the confused voices and anguished cries, the search for
    what is real,
you come, risen Lord, to still tongues and speak our name.
You cannot be held on to, controlled or manipulated;
you come by your own grace and in your own time.
Be our teacher this day.
Lead us to your Father, your God,
your truth, your life,
that we may say with Mary,
'I have seen the Lord'
and carry that word
to a world desperate for true peace and real hope.

36   Sent out

John 20:19–23

Jesus said to them again, 'Peace be with you. As the Father has sent me, so I send you.'

JOHN 20:21

When we hide behind locked doors,
fearful of the world with all its horrors and needs,
meet us, risen Lord Jesus, and speak your peace.
Then breathe your Spirit deep into the centre of our being;
drive out our fear and shame.
Send us out into the world you so love,
carrying your forgiveness, compassion and hope.
Send us out, this and every day,
filled with your breath, makers of peace.

37   Living trust

John 20:24–31

'Blessed are those who have not seen and yet have come to believe.'
JOHN 20:29

Risen Jesus, my Lord and my God,
I do not see
your presence with me,
your victory for the world,
love overcoming hatred,
and life instead of death.
I do not see:
my sight is poor;
my vision is weak.
But with the help of the gospel
and your Spirit at work within me,
I will believe.
I will put my trust in you,
and believing, here and now,
I receive your overflowing life,
abundant and eternal,
a life given in love for the world.

38   It is the Lord

John 21:1–14

Jesus said to them, 'Come and have breakfast.' Now none of the disciples dared to ask him, 'Who are you?' because they knew it was the Lord.

JOHN 21:12

It is the Lord, standing there beside the water,
looking into our eyes.
It is the Lord, beckoning us to go and fish once more,
to forget all that now lies in the past.
It is the Lord, calling us to walk his way,
to do his kingdom work.
It is the Lord, inviting us to share food and know his blessing,
to know his presence, the bread of life, and his grace.
It is the Lord, calling us every day to journey with him,
to speak our needs, to share our joys and our pains,
to offer our thanks and to offer lives,
knowing that with us every step, it is the Lord,
there to the end of time and beyond.

39   Do you love me?

John 21:15–19

When they had finished breakfast, Jesus said to Simon Peter, 'Simon son of John, do you love me more than these?'
JOHN 21:15

God who meets us in Jesus,
love was your starting point as you drew Peter back to your way,
echoing his threefold denial with your questions.
So we too must bring love to all that we do in your name:
love as we look back on the ways
we have denied and deserted you;
love as we feel the pain of your searching questions;
love as we play our part in caring for your people today;
love as we look to the future, whatever it may bring;
love as we seek not to compare
and contrast ourselves with others
but simply, honestly and thankfully to follow you.
Help us to grow in love for you and for the world you so love.

40 The story continues

John 21:20–31

But there are also many other things that Jesus did; if every one of them were written down, I suppose that the world itself could not contain the books that would be written.
JOHN 21: 25

Continue your story, living, life-giving Jesus
in the lives of your followers,
in forgiveness found and love outpoured.
Continue your story, in our world today,
with all its wonder and grief, hope and terror.
Continue your story in surprising people and unexpected places,
in lives lived and given and renewed.
Continue your story, breaking the limits we place upon it,
that it may be told in countless ways and lives.
Continue your story, to the glory of God,
who was, and is and is to come,
the ever-loving, ever-living, everlasting one.

Appendix: A pattern for prayer

You may wish to use the following pattern of prayer that draws from the four gospels to provide the setting for your reading and praying the way. It can be used very flexibly. The pattern is simple enough that it – and some of the key verses – can be memorised and so can be used when walking if that is more helpful. While written for individual use, the pattern can also be used with a prayer partner or small group. It is important that you adapt to your own needs, situation and personality, while not avoiding the real challenge that such gospel praying brings.

The constant pressure on us is to go for a quick fix in prayer and to fail to recognise the patience and persistence required to wait on God and to listen. Quietening our minds and stilling our bodies is an important part of preparing to pray – that going into your own room and shutting the door that Jesus describes in the sermon on the mount (Matthew 6:6). But prayer is never simply down to us. It is not some anxiety-ridden striving after the invisible, but a conversation with one who knows our needs and our hearts. Jesus often confronts the disciples' anxieties and, again in the sermon on the mount, tells his disciples not to try to impress God with long prayers: 'your Father knows what you need before you ask him' (Matthew 6:8). Prayer is a meeting of human boldness – the persistence to continue to speak to God, whatever we may feel – and God's grace – the patient loving-kindness of God for us all, come what may.

1 Preparing to pray

Enter God's presence in stillness, remembering Jesus is beside you and seeking the help of the Spirit within you. Enter the room of God's presence, shutting the door behind you.

Prayer *(may be repeated)*:

> Emmanuel – God is with us (Matthew 1:23).
> *or* Blessed be the one who comes in the name of the Lord (Mark 11:9).
> *or* Glory to God in the highest and peace on earth (Luke 2:14).
> *or* It is the Spirit that gives life (John 6:63).

2 Seeking God's mercy

Reflect on the ways in which you have distanced yourself from God, drawn back from love for God and neighbour:

> Hear O Israel: the Lord our God, the Lord is one; you shall love the Lord your God with all your heart, and with all your soul, and with all your mind, and with all your strength... You shall love your neighbour as yourself.
> MARK 12:29–31

Prayer *(may be repeated)*:

> Lord, have mercy on me, a sinner (Luke 18:13).

Assurance: Jesus says, 'Friend, your sins are forgiven' (Luke 5:20).

You may wish to use one of Luke's canticles of praise:

- The Benedictus (Luke 1:68–79)
- The Magnificat (Luke 1:46b–55)

3   Hearing the gospel

*Read the gospel passage and be opened by the Spirit to God's word,
made known in the story of Jesus:*

The Word became flesh and lived among us… full of grace
and truth.
JOHN 1:14

4   Giving thanks and praying for others

Enter a time of prayer:

Father, I thank you… *(name causes of thanksgiving)*
Father, forgive… *(name people you need to forgive)*
Father, into your hands I commit… *(name people and situations
in need of God's peace, justice or healing)*

5   Sharing the Abba prayer

*Join all Jesus' followers in praying a version of the Lord's Prayer
(in words familiar to you or in one of the versions below):*

Abba, Father, not what I want, but what you want (Mark 14:36).

or

Father, may your name be hallowed;
your kingdom come.
Give us each day our daily bread.
And forgive us our sins,
for we too forgive all who have done us wrong.
And do not put us to the test.
LUKE 11:2–4 (REB)

or

Our Father in heaven,
    hallowed be your name.
    Your kingdom come.
    Your will be done,
        on earth as it is in heaven.
    Give us this day our daily bread.
    And forgive us our debts,
        as we also have forgiven our debtors.
    And do not bring us to the time of trial,
        but rescue us from the evil one.
MATTHEW 6:9–13

or

Father, glorify your name.
JOHN 12:28

You may wish to use another of Luke's canticles:

- Song of Simeon (Luke 2:29–32)

6   Concluding prayer

Use a closing prayer, such as:

Lord Jesus,
increase our faith,
renew our love,
deepen our joy,
for the sake of the kingdom.
based on LUKE 17:5

7   Final reflection

End by reflecting on one of the following verses:

Christ came not to be served but to serve and to give his life
for me and for many (Mark 10:45).
I was lost but now am found; I was dead but now am alive
(Luke 15:32).
Jesus says, 'I am with you always, to the end of time'
(Matthew 28:20).
Jesus says, 'Peace be with you. As the Father has sent me,
so I send you' (John 20:21).

Thanks be to God.

*Move out of praying, recognising the touch and blessing of God on
your life.*

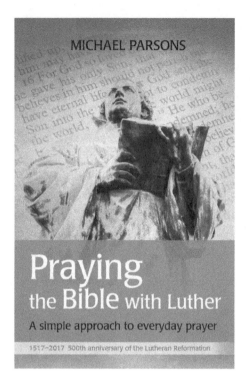

There is a need in today's church to relate scripture and prayer in such a way as to enable us to speak God's words after him. This book takes a simple lectio divina approach developed in the 16th century by Martin Luther and offers practical guidance to pray in this way.

Praying the Bible with Luther
A simple approach to everyday prayer
Michael Parsons
978 0 85746 503 0 £7.99

brfonline.org.uk